# BUSINESS
# FRENCH

A QUICK BEGINNER'S COURSE FOR BUSINESS PEOPLE

● MONIQUE JONES ●

**BBC BOOKS**

Published by BBC Books
a division of BBC Enterprises Ltd
Woodlands, 80 Wood Lane
London W12 0TT

First published 1993

© Monique Jones 1993

Audio producer: Colette Thomson
Footstep Productions Ltd

ISBN 0 563 36473 4
Map and illustrations by Julian Bingley
Cover illustration by Nick Sharratt

Set in Great Britain by
Goodfellow & Egan Phototypesetting Ltd, Cambridge
Printed and bound in Great Britain by Clays Ltd, St Ives Plc
Cover printed by Clays Ltd, St Ives Plc

Exclusive U.S. Distributor of the Get By in Series Packs

Ambrose Video Publishing Inc.
1290 Avenue of the Americas
Suite 2245, New York, N.Y. 10104

# CONTENTS

# INTRODUCTION

The BBC *Get by in business French* is a six-unit course for anyone planning to do business with a French-speaking country. It provides a basic 'survival kit' for some of the situations you are likely to find yourself in.

*Get by in business French* is especially designed for those who have little or no knowledge of French, so that they can get more enjoyment out of their business trips abroad. The course consists of two self-contained audiocassettes and this book.

The audiocassettes concentrate on what you'll need to say and understand to cope with particular situations – getting somewhere, booking in to a hotel, making appointments on the phone, introducing yourself, your firm and your products and services . . . They include everyday and business conversations right from the start and give you opportunities to repeat the words and phrases you hear and to work out for yourself how to 'get by'.

The *Get by* book is divided into six sections, each comprising five elements:

- the key words and phrases you'll need to follow the dialogues;

- the texts of the recorded dialogues;

- explanations of the language used and exercises for you to practise what you've learnt;

- some background information you may find useful when doing business with French-speaking people;

- a self-assessment exercise to let you know how you are progressing.

At the back of the book, you'll find a useful Reference section including a pronunciation guide, numbers, the key to the exercises and a French-English vocabulary list.

# TO MAKE THE MOST OF THE COURSE

- Always start by listening carefully to the tape. Listen to each unit section by section. Each section consists of key words and phrases, a dialogue (sometimes two) and explanations and exercises. Join in the exercises as you go along.

- Read the key words and phrases for the section and listen to the tape again as many times as you like.

- Then read the explanations and do the exercises to try out what you've been learning. Keys are at the back of the book. The headphone symbol indicates dialogues on the tape and exercises that require you to listen to the tape.

- When you have completed all the sections in the unit, read Worth Knowing.

- Complete the self-assessment table to give yourself an idea of how you are doing.

It's a good idea to practise with someone else if possible. For pronunciation practice use the tape. At the end of the second cassette, there is a recording of all the words in the pronunciation guide at the end of this book, with pauses for you to repeat them. If you have recording facilities, record and compare yourself to the original.

Good luck with your business French . . . *Bon courage!*

# ● THE REGIONS OF FRANCE ●

| Region | Capital | Industries |
|---|---|---|
| Alsace | Strasbourg | European administrations |
| Aquitaine | Bordeaux | Paper; wine |
| Auvergne | Clermont-Ferrand | Tyres |
| Bourgogne | Dijon | Wine |
| Bretagne | Rennes | Agro-food industry |
| Centre | Orléans | Jardin de la France |
| Champagne-Ardenne | Châlons sur Marne | Champagne |
| Corse | Ajaccio | Agriculture; tourism |
| Franche-Comté | Besançon | Precision engineering |
| Île-de-France | Paris | All sectors |
| Languedoc-Roussillon | Montpellier | Tourism; bio-medical; robotics |
| Limousin | Limoges | Agriculture; porcelain |
| Lorraine | Metz | Steel; coal |
| Midi-Pyrénées | Toulouse | Aerospace; high tech |
| Nord-Pas-de-Calais | Lille | Steel; textiles |
| Basse-Normandie | Caen | Agriculture; tourism |
| Haute-Normandie | Rouen | Cosmetics; pharmaceuticals |
| Pays de la Loire | Nantes | Cars; agro-food |
| Picardie | Amiens | Textiles |
| Poitou-Charentes | Poitiers | Cognac; insurance |
| Provence-Alpes-Côte d'Azur | Marseille | Petrochemicals; high tech; tourism |
| Rhône-Alpes | Lyon | Gastronomy in Lyon; high tech in Grenoble |

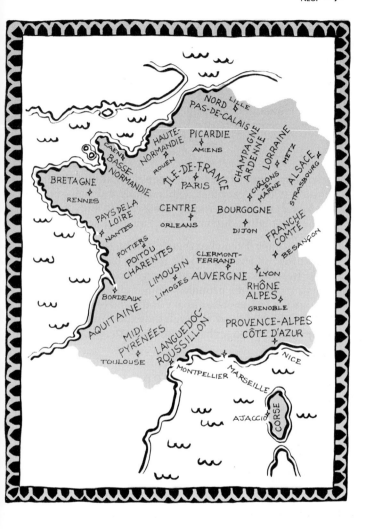

# ┃ GETTING THERE

## ● TASK ●

Start by listening to the first section of this unit – At the airport – with its exercises, explanations and dialogues. Join in the exercises as you go along. Don't look at the book except when instructed to do an exercise.

After you have listened to this section on the tape study the key words and phrases and the relevant dialogues in the book. Read them aloud as often as you can. Use the cassette to check the pronunciation. You may want to read through the language summary at the end of the book. You should then work through the explanations and complete the exercises before going on to the next section.

## ● AT THE AIRPORT ●

| **KEY WORDS AND PHRASES** | |
|---|---|
| **pardon/excusez-moi** | excuse me |
| **oui** | yes |
| **non** | no |
| **pour les bagages?** | where is the luggage? |
| **s'il vous plaît** | please |
| **merci** | thank you |
| **là-bas** | over there/there |
| **livraison des bagages** | luggage collection/delivery |
| **continuez tout droit** | continue straight on |

| | |
|---|---|
| **la sortie** | exit |
| **à gauche** | on the left |
| **à droite** | on the right |
| **en face** | opposite |
| **la navette RER** | the RER shuttle |
| **devant** | in front (of) |

## 1–1 At the airport

### 1 🎧 LOOKING FOR YOUR LUGGAGE

| | |
|---|---|
| M. LAYEN | Pardon monsieur. |
| PASSANT | Oui? |
| M. LAYEN | Pour les bagages s'il vous plaît? |
| PASSANT | Là-bas. Livraison des bagages. |
| M. LAYEN | Merci monsieur. |

### 2 🎧 LOOKING FOR THE RER (RÉSEAU EXPRESS RÉGIONAL) STATION

| | |
|---|---|
| M. LAYEN | Excusez-moi madame, pour le RER s'il vous plaît? |
| PASSANTE | Le RER? Continuez tout droit, sortie 31 à gauche en face des toilettes. |
| M. LAYEN | Oui. |
| PASSANTE | La navette RER est devant la sortie 31, à droite. |
| M. LAYEN | Merci madame. |

### EXPLANATIONS AND EXERCISES

**Masculine, feminine and plural**

In French all nouns are either masculine or feminine whether they are people, animals or things. It is better to learn the gender of each word as you go along. The words for 'the', 'a', 'an' and 'some' change according to the gender of the noun they are attached to:

| Masculine | Feminine | Plural (masc. & fem.) |
|:---:|:---:|:---:|
| *le, l'*<br>the | *la, l'*<br>the | *les*<br>the |
| *un*<br>a, an | *une*<br>a, an | *des*<br>some |

You learn *le billet*, *le ticket* but *la sortie* and *les toilettes*, *les bagages*. *L'* is used instead of *le* or *la* in front of a word starting with a vowel or an *h–* (*l'aéroport*, *l'hôpital*).

There are also two words for 'a' or 'an': *un ticket*, *une sortie*.

Nouns seldom stand alone in French, so look out for the frequent use of *des* meaning 'some': *des sorties* for '(some) exits.'

### Numbers
Numbers are important in order to understand prices, time and directions. To ask people to repeat them just say: *répétez s'il vous plaît*. To ask them to slow down, say: *lentement s'il vous plaît* or *plus lentement s'il vous plaît*.

| 1 | 2 | 3 | 4 | 5 | 6 | 7 | 8 | 9 | 10 |
|---|---|---|---|---|---|---|---|---|---|
| un | deux | trois | quatre | cinq | six | sept | huit | neuf | dix |

| 100 | 200 | 300 | 400 |
|---|---|---|---|
| cent | deux cents | trois cents | quatre cents |

### Asking where things are
The simplest way to ask where something is is to name it and then to say 'please':

*Le bureau de change s'il vous plaît?*
*Les toilettes s'il vous plaît?*

You can also start with *pour*:
*Pour les bagages s'il vous plaît?*
*Pour le RER s'il vous plaît?*

To stop a passer-by (*passant/passante*) for information, use:
*Pardon monsieur* . . .
*Excusez-moi madame* . . .

Another useful expression to ask where places are, is *c'est où* (where is it?):
*Le RER, c'est où?*
*C'est où la navette, s'il vous plaît?*

To ask quite simply 'where is' something, you say *où est?*:
*Où est la sortie?*

## Directions

*c'est*  it is
*là-bas*  over there
*à droite*  right
*sur la droite*  on the right
*à gauche*  left
*sur la gauche*  on the left
*tout droit*  straight on
*en face des toilettes*  opposite the toilets
*devant la sortie*  in front of the exit
*devant la porte*  in front of the gate/door

🎧 **EXERCISE 1–1**
This exercise is recorded. Although the text is written out below, hide it and do the exercise first as a listening comprehension.

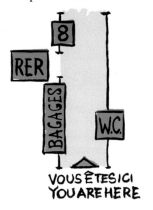

Can you find out where you are going?

**a**  Continuez tout droit, c'est à droite.

**b**  Continuez tout droit, c'est à gauche en face des WC.

**c**  Continuez tout droit, c'est devant la sortie huit.

# ● BUYING RER AND TRAIN TICKETS ●

## KEY WORDS AND PHRASES

| | |
|---|---|
| **un ticket pour** | a ticket to (underground) |
| **première/deuxième classe** | first/second class |
| **voilà** | there you are/it is |
| **c'est direct?** | is it a direct line? |
| **changez à** | change at/in |
| **prenez** | take |
| **la ligne** | the line |
| **pouvez-vous répeter s'il vous plaît** | could you repeat, please |
| **lentement s'il vous plaît** | slowly please |
| **direction** | towards |
| **TGV (train à grande vitesse)** | high speed train |
| **un billet** | a ticket (train) |
| **un aller simple** | a single (ticket) |
| **un aller-retour** | a return (ticket) |
| **fumeur/non fumeur** | smoker/non-smoker |
| **quel train?** | which train? |
| **le train de seize heures quatorze** | the 16.14 train |
| **la voiture** | carriage |
| **la place** | seat |
| **c'est combien?** | how much is it? |
| **alors** | then/well |

## 1–2 At the RER station

🎧 A TICKET TO . . .

| | |
|---|---|
| M. LAYEN | Un ticket pour La Défense s'il vous plaît. |
| EMPLOYÉ | Première ou deuxième classe? |
| M. LAYEN | Deuxième. |
| EMPLOYÉ | Voilà monsieur, trente-neuf francs cinquante. |
| M. LAYEN | Merci monsieur. C'est direct? |
| EMPLOYÉ | Non monsieur, changez à Châtelet Les Halles, prenez la ligne RER A, direction Saint Germain. |
| M. LAYEN | Merci monsieur. |

## 1–3 At the Gare de Lyon: travelling by TGV

1 🎧 BUYING A TICKET

| | |
|---|---|
| M. LAYEN | Un billet pour Lyon s'il vous plaît. |
| EMPLOYÉE | Un aller simple ou un aller-retour? |
| M. LAYEN | Un aller simple. |
| EMPLOYÉE | Première ou deuxième classe? |
| M. LAYEN | Deuxième. |
| EMPLOYÉE | Fumeur ou non fumeur? |
| M. LAYEN | Non fumeur. |

2 🎧 BOOKING A SEAT (LA RÉSA)

| | |
|---|---|
| EMPLOYÉE | Quel train? |
| M. LAYEN | Le train de seize heures quatorze. |
| EMPLOYÉE | Alors voiture douze, place vingt. |
| M. LAYEN | C'est combien? |
| EMPLOYÉE | Deux cent soixante francs. |
| M. LAYEN | Voilà madame. |

## More numbers

| 11 | 12 | 13 | 14 | 15 |
|---|---|---|---|---|
| onze | douze | treize | quatorze | quinze |

| 16 | 17 | 18 | 19 | 20 |
|---|---|---|---|---|
| seize | dix-sept | dix-huit | dix-neuf | vingt |

| 21 | 22 | 23 | 30 |
|---|---|---|---|
| vingt et un | vingt-deux | vingt-trois | trente |

| 40 | 50 | 60 |
|---|---|---|
| quarante | cinquante | soixante |

## Ordinal numbers (first, second . . .)

'First' is (*le*) *premier* for a masculine word, and (*la*) *première* for a feminine word.

Otherwise just add *-ième* to the number: *deux**ième** (le/la deuxième)*, *trois**ième** (le/la troisième)*, *dix**ième** (le/la dixième)*, etc.

However numbers ending with an *-e* drop that *-e* before adding *-ième*: *quatre* becomes *quatrième*, *douze* becomes *douzième*.

*Vingt et un*, *trente et un*, and so on become *vingt et unième*, *trente et unième*.
Finally the *-f* in *neuf* becomes a *-v-*: *neuvième*, *dix-neuvième*.

### More directions
*la première à droite*   first right
*la deuxième/seconde à gauche*   second left
*prenez*   take
*continuez*   continue
*prenez la troisième à droite*   take the third on the right

🎧   EXERCISE 1–2

This exercise is recorded. Although the text is written out below, hide it and do the exercise first as a listening comprehension.

Follow the instructions and find out where you are going:
**a**   Continuez tout droit et c'est à gauche.
**b**   Prenez la première à droite puis la première à droite et c'est à gauche.
**c**   Prenez la deuxième à droite puis la troisième à droite et c'est sur la gauche.
**d**   Prenez la première à droite puis la deuxième à gauche, continuez tout droit et c'est en face.

## The time

For business and official timetables, the French use the 24 hour clock; it is also frequently used in everyday speech.
*Quelle heure est-il?*    What time is it?
*Il est*    It is

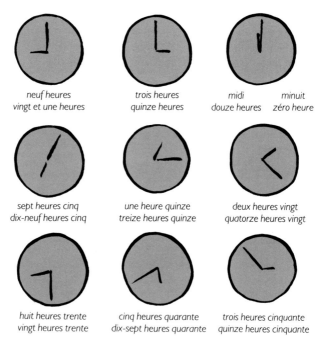

| | | |
|:---:|:---:|:---:|
| *neuf heures*<br>*vingt et une heures* | *trois heures*<br>*quinze heures* | *midi*    *minuit*<br>*douze heures*  *zéro heure* |
| *sept heures cinq*<br>*dix-neuf heures cinq* | *une heure quinze*<br>*treize heures quinze* | *deux heures vingt*<br>*quatorze heures vingt* |
| *huit heures trente*<br>*vingt heures trente* | *cinq heures quarante*<br>*dix-sept heures quarante* | *trois heures cinquante*<br>*quinze heures cinquante* |

🎧    **EXERCISE 1–3**

Listen to the different times and match them with these:

**a** 8.05    **b** 13.15    **c** 21.40    **d** 00.52    **e** 18.00

You could also write them in words and practise saying them, checking your pronunciation with the tape.

## Buying tickets

A ticket is *un ticket* for the RER and Métro (Underground)

but *un billet* for the train, whether normal or high speed.
*un ticket pour/un billet pour*   a ticket to

You will be asked to choose between:
*un aller simple ou un aller-retour?*   a single or a return?
*première ou seconde classe?*   first or second class?
*fumeur ou non fumeur?*   smoker or non-smoker?

And for the train:
*quel train?*   which train?
*le train de onze heures*   the 11.00 train

For the TGV you are given two tickets: *le billet*, which is
for the journey between two towns and is at a fixed price,
and *la Résa* which is to book a seat on a particular train
between these two towns. The price of the *Résa* varies with
the time of the day and year.

## Prices
To ask how much things cost you can say:
*C'est combien?*   How much is it?
*Ça fait combien?*   How much is it?
*Je vous dois combien?*   How much do I owe you?

You will notice that in French the comma is used to mark
the decimal point: you write *9,50F* but you say *neuf francs
cinquante*. A full stop is used between the thousands: you
write *10.000F* and you say *dix mille francs*.
*Ça fait quatre cents francs*   It is/it comes to 400 francs

🎧   **EXERCISE 1–4**
Listen to conversation 1–3 again to find out:

**a**   where monsieur Layen is going
**b**   whether he wants a single or a return
**c**   if he travels first class
**d**   if he smokes
**e**   at what time his train leaves
**f**   which carriage and seat he is given
**g**   how much his journey costs

You could also complete this exercise from the text of
conversation 1–3 on page 15.

# • ARRIVING AT YOUR HOTEL •

| KEY WORDS AND PHRASES | |
|---|---|
| **j'ai réservé une chambre** | I have booked a room |
| **une chambre à un lit** | a single room |
| **avec douche** | with shower |
| **pour une nuit** | for one night |
| **c'est ça/c'est bien ça** | that's right |
| **voici la clé** | here is the key |
| **chambre dix-sept** | room seventeen |
| **à quelle heure servez-vous?** | at what time do you serve? |
| **le petit-déjeuner** | breakfast |
| **de . . . à . . .** | from . . . to . . . |
| **pourriez-vous?** | could you? |
| **me réveiller à** | call/wake me at? |
| **bien sûr** | certainly/of course |
| **bonjour** | good morning/afternoon |
| **bonsoir** | good evening |
| **bonne nuit** | good night |

## 1–4 Arriving at the hotel

| 1 🎧 | I HAVE BOOKED A ROOM |
|---|---|
| GÉRANT | Bonsoir monsieur. |
| M. LAYEN | Bonsoir. J'ai réservé une chambre. Monsieur Layen. |
| GÉRANT | Oui, monsieur Layen . . . Voilà. Une chambre à un lit avec douche pour une nuit. |
| M. LAYEN | C'est bien ça. |
| GÉRANT | Voici la clé. Chambre dix-sept. |

## 2 🎧 AT WHAT TIME DO YOU SERVE BREAKFAST?

| | |
|---|---|
| M. LAYEN | A quelle heure servez-vous le petit-déjeuner? |
| GÉRANT | De sept heures à neuf heures trente, monsieur. |
| M. LAYEN | Pourriez-vous me réveiller à sept heures quinze s'il vous plaît? |
| GÉRANT | Bien sûr monsieur. |
| M. LAYEN | Merci monsieur. Bonsoir. |
| GÉRANT | Bonne nuit monsieur. |

### EXPLANATIONS AND EXERCISES

### Checking in
To check in at your hotel:
*J'ai réservé une chambre*   I have booked a room
*J'ai une réservation*   I have got a booking

To give your name, you can just say *monsieur* or *madame*
followed by your surname, or you could use the
following:
*Je suis monsieur Smith*   I am Mr Smith
*Je m'appelle madame Smith*   My name is Mrs Smith
*au nom de Smith*   in the name of Smith

### Types of room
To specify the kind of room you have booked:
*une chambre à un lit*   a single room
*une chambre à deux lits*   a twin-bedded room
*une chambre à grand lit*   a double room
*avec douche*   with shower
*avec bain*   with bath

To describe the duration of the stay, simply use *pour*
followed by the number of nights:
*pour trois nuits*   for three nights

### Breakfast and a morning call
To know at what time breakfast is served you ask:
*A quelle heure servez-vous le petit-déjeuner?*

The likely answers are:
*de sept heures à neuf heures*   from 7 am to 9 am
*à partir de sept heures*   from 7 am
*jusqu'à neuf heures*   up to/until 9 am

For a morning call, you could say:
*Pourriez-vous me réveiller à?*   Could you call me at?
*à six heures et demie*   at 6.30 am

### Greetings

*Bonjour* is used for 'good morning' and 'good afternoon'.
*Bonsoir* is used for 'good evening' and sometimes as
'goodbye' in the evening.
*Au revoir* means 'goodbye' at any time.
*Bonne nuit* is the equivalent of 'good night'.
As for *merci* and *pardon*, they are often followed by
*monsieur, madame* or *mademoiselle*.
If it is someone you know you can add their name:
*Bonjour monsieur Layen*
*Mademoiselle* should only be used if you know the person is
single. It is an insult to call a married lady *mademoiselle*.

### EXERCISE 1–5

You have just arrived at your hotel and you have to book
in. Fill in your side of the conversation in French using the
English line as a guide.

| | |
|---|---|
| RÉCEPTIONNISTE | Bonsoir monsieur. |
| YOU | *Greet her, and tell her you have booked a room in your name.* |
| RÉCEPTIONNISTE | Ah oui, voilà. C'est bien une chambre à un lit avec douche pour quatre nuits? |
| YOU | *That's right.* |
| RÉCEPTIONNISTE | Voici la clé, chambre dix-huit. |
| YOU | *Ask her at what time breakfast is served.* |
| RÉCEPTIONNISTE | De sept heures à neuf heures quinze, monsieur. |
| YOU | *Ask her if she could give you a morning call at 6.30 am.* |

| | |
|---|---|
| RÉCEPTIONNISTE | Bien sûr monsieur. |
| YOU | *Thank her and say goodnight.* |
| RÉCEPTIONNISTE | Bonne nuit monsieur. |

**WORTH KNOWING**

## Travelling by public transport

In order to find your way around you will need to recognise the following signs:

 Underground (*le Métro*)

 Fast city and suburban railway (*le Réseau Express Régional*)

 Bus stop

 Train station

## From Roissy to Paris

From the Charles de Gaulle airport in Roissy, there are two easy ways of getting into Paris, apart from taking a taxi:

- the Air France coach departs for Etoile every twelve minutes. The journey takes one hour.
- by RER (*Réseau Express Régional*). The shuttle to the RER station operates every five minutes from terminal 1. A ticket costs 29 francs to go to the Gare du Nord or 39,50 francs to La Défense. Look out for the connections with the Métro network.

## Parisian public transport

The RATP (*Régie Autonome des Transports Parisiens*) runs the Underground network (*le Métro*), the buses and part of the RER (which is the equivalent of, say, Network South-East). The same tickets are used to travel on the Métro, buses and the inner-Paris part of the RER (*section urbaine*).

They can be bought at any Underground station singly
(6 francs) or in tens (ask for a *carnet*, 36,50 francs) from the
ticket offices or machines. They are also sold at bus garages
and at some newsagents.

### The SNCF

The SNCF (*Société Nationale des Chemins de fer Français*) is
France's railway network. Trains are comfortable and
generally on time. For speed choose the TGV (*train à grande
vitesse*), France's high speed train. You will need to buy a
ticket for the journey and book a seat on a particular train
with a *Résa TGV*, for which you will pay a small fee.

You must validate (*composter*) tickets and *Résa* in the orange
machines which are in the hall in front of the entrance to
the platforms.

### SELF-ASSESSMENT

You will get a rough idea of how well you are doing by
ticking the following statements:

| I can | from memory (A) | with some reference to the text (B) | with full support (C) |
|---|---|---|---|
| ask for directions | | | |
| understand directions | | | |
| buy a ticket | | | |
| count to sixty | | | |
| understand the time | | | |
| book into a hotel | | | |
| ask for a morning call | | | |

If you have ticked mainly A you are doing well. If there
are quite a few Cs you'd better take your book with you.

# 2 INTRODUCTIONS

## ● TASK ●

In this unit you will learn to get through to the right person when telephoning to make or change an appointment and to introduce yourself and your company when visiting a potential client. Here again you will learn ready-made sentences rather than vocabulary. In the answers the language might be more elaborate, you must therefore concentrate on the key words so as to understand the important information.

## ● GETTING THROUGH TO THE RIGHT PERSON ●

| KEY WORDS AND PHRASES | |
|---|---|
| le/la standardiste | switchboard operator |
| allô | hallo (phone) |
| ici M. Smith/M. Smith à l'appareil | Mr Smith speaking |
| je voudrais | I would like |
| je voudrais parler à | I would like to speak to |
| ne quittez pas | hold on |
| je vous passe | I'll put you through to |
| le service des achats | the buying department |
| la secrétaire de Mme Blois | Mrs Blois' secretary |
| malheureusement | unfortunately |
| est en réunion | is at a meeting |

| | |
|---|---|
| **quand** | when |
| **puis-je la joindre?** | can I reach her |
| **après** | after |
| **bien** | well |
| **je rappellerai** | I'll call back |

## 2–1 I would like to speak to

### 1 🎧 GETTING THROUGH TO THE SWITCH BOARD

STANDARDISTE  Allô, la société Europas, bonjour.
M. LAYEN  Je voudrais parler à madame Blois.
STANDARDISTE  Ne quittez pas, je vous passe le service des achats.

### 2 🎧 GETTING THROUGH TO THE SECRETARY

SECRÉTAIRE  Allô, la secrétaire de madame Blois à l'appareil.
M. LAYEN  Allô, bonjour madame, je voudrais parler à madame Blois s'il vous plaît.
SECRÉTAIRE  Malheureusement madame Blois est en réunion.
M. LAYEN  Quand puis-je la joindre?
SECRÉTAIRE  Après quatorze heures.
M. LAYEN  Bien je rappellerai après quatorze heures. Au revoir madame.
SECRÉTAIRE  Au revoir monsieur.

### EXPLANATIONS AND EXERCISES

### Asking for someone
*Je voudrais parler à*  I would like to speak to
*Puis-je parler à . . . ?*  Could I speak to . . . ?

## To find out when you can get in touch with someone
*Quand puis-je la joindre?*   When can I reach her?
*Quand puis-je le contacter?*   When can I contact him?

## To say when you will call back
*Je rappellerai après onze heures*   I'll call back after 11 am
*Je rappellerai à partir de onze heures*   I'll call back from
11 am on

## When answering the phone
*Allô* followed by the name of the company:

*Allô, la société Europas*

People use *ici* in front of their name or *à l'appareil* after their
name:
*Allô, ici Monique Blois*
*Allô, la secrétaire de madame Blois à l'appareil*   Mrs Blois'
secretary speaking

## To transfer someone
*La ligne est occupée*   the line is engaged
*Ne quittez pas*  ⎫
*Patientez*       ⎬ *hold on*
*Restez en ligne* ⎭
*Je vous le passe*   I'll transfer you (where you're being
transferred to a man)
*Je vous la passe*   I'll transfer you (to a lady)
*Je vous passe le service des achats*   I'll transfer you to the
buying department

## To say someone is at a meeting
*malheureusement*   unfortunately
*je regrette*   I am sorry/I regret
*je suis désolé*   I am sorry
*Madame Blois est en réunion*   Mrs Blois is at a meeting
*Monsieur Layen est en conférence*   Mr Layen is at a
conference/meeting

**EXERCISE 2–1**

You are trying to contact monsieur Vardon, who is at a meeting.

Fill in your side of the conversation.

| | |
|---|---|
| STANDARDISTE | Allô, la société Avantis, bonjour. |
| YOU | *Ask to speak to monsieur Vardon.* |
| STANDARDISTE | Ne quittez pas, je vous passe le service des achats . . . |
| EMPLOYÉ | Allô, ici le service des achats. |
| YOU | *Ask to speak to monsieur Vardon.* |
| EMPLOYÉ | Je regrette, monsieur Vardon est en réunion. |
| YOU | *Ask when you can reach him.* |
| EMPLOYÉ | Après quinze heures. |
| YOU | *Say you will call back after 3 pm.* |
| EMPLOYÉ | Très bien, au revoir monsieur. |
| YOU | *Thank him and say good bye.* |

# • INTRODUCTIONS AND APPOINTMENTS •

| KEY WORDS AND PHRASES | |
|---:|---|
| **je suis** | I am |
| **le chef des ventes** | sales manager |
| **je voudrais** | I would like |
| **un rendez-vous** | an appointment |
| **pour vous présenter** | to present to you |
| **nos produits** | our products |
| **la semaine prochaine** | next week |
| **mardi matin** | Tuesday morning |
| **je suis libre/disponible** | I am free/available |
| **c'est parfait** | OK |
| **à mardi** | see you on Tuesday |

## 2–2 I would like an appointment

| 🎧 | I AM |
|---|---|

| | |
|---|---|
| MME BLOIS | Allô, ici Monique Blois. |
| M. LAYEN | Bonjour madame, je suis Joseph Layen, chef des ventes de la compagnie Norma. |
| MME BLOIS | Bonjour monsieur. |
| M. LAYEN | Je voudrais un rendez-vous pour vous présenter nos produits. |
| MME BLOIS | D'accord. La semaine prochaine . . . oui, mardi matin je suis libre à onze heures. |
| M. LAYEN | Alors, mardi onze heures, c'est parfait. Merci madame, au revoir. |
| MME BLOIS | Au revoir monsieur et à mardi. |

### EXPLANATIONS AND EXERCISES

**To introduce yourself**
*Je suis Joseph Layen*   I am Joseph Layen
*Je m'appelle Monique Blois*   My name is Monique Blois

**To state your position**
*Je suis chef des ventes*   I am the sales manager
*Je suis chef des achats*   I am the purchasing manager

(There is a list of different functions in the Worth Knowing section.)

**To state the company**
*de la compagnie Norma*          *de la firme Schopp*
*de la société Thomson*          *des établissements Duros*
*de l'entreprise Aribas*

'From' and 'of the' are translated by:

| Masculine | Feminine | Word starting (with a vowel) | Plural |
|---|---|---|---|
| *du*<br>du service | *de la*<br>de la société | *de l'*<br>de l'entreprise | *des*<br>des établissements |

## The days of the week
In France the week starts on Monday:

---
lundi mardi mercredi jeudi vendredi samedi dimanche

---

All the days are masculine and do not take a capital letter.
*lundi*   on Monday (in French 'on' is omitted)
*le lundi*   on Mondays
*mardi prochain*   next Tuesday
*mardi dernier*   last Tuesday
*les jours de la semaine*   the days of the week
*la semaine prochaine*   next week
*la semaine dernière*   last week

## Adjectives: their place and the feminine form
Most adjectives come after the noun they qualify: *mardi*
**prochain**.

For the feminine form of most adjectives, add an *-e*:
*le mois prochain* (next month) but *la semaine prochain**e***
*le mois dernier* but *la semaine derni**è**r**e*** (you also need to add
an accent to make *dernière*)
*le mois suivant* (the following month) but *la semaine suivant**e***.

## Agreeing with someone
The simplest way is to say *oui*. But there are lots of
variations.

*d'accord*   OK
*(très) bien madame*   (very) well
*bien sûr monsieur*   of course
*tout à fait*   Ok/that's right
*c'est bien ça/c'est ça*   that's right
*c'est parfait*   Ok/fine/perfect
*avec plaisir*   with pleasure

**EXERCISE 2–2**

How would you say the following sentences in French?

**a**  I am Roger Vadim, Ferguson's sales manager.
**b**  I would like an appointment.
**c**  I would like to present our products to you.
**d**  OK, next Friday I am free at 2 pm.
**e**  Goodbye, see you on Thursday.

## ● CHANGING AN APPOINTMENT ●

Mr Layen wants to change an appointment with one of his long-standing customers but the date he proposes is not convenient. Notice how they are less formal when greeting each other.

| KEY WORDS AND PHRASES | |
|---:|:---|
| comment allez-vous? | how are you? |
| (très) bien | (very) well |
| et vous? | and you? |
| ça va | fine/OK/well |
| mais | but |
| • je ne peux pas | I can't |
| je ne peux pas venir | I can't come |
| comme prévu | as planned |
| est-ce qu'on pourrait . . . ? | could we . . . ? |
| remettre | delay |
| attendez | wait/a moment |
| c'est impossible | it's impossible |
| je ne suis pas libre | I am not free |
| donc | then/therefore |
| je vous en prie | you're welcome |

## 2–3 I would like to delay

| I 🎧 | GREETINGS |
|---|---|

| | |
|---|---|
| M. NOBIS | Allô, ici Marc Nobis. |
| M. LAYEN | Bonjour Marc, Joseph Layen à l'appareil, comment allez-vous? |
| M. NOBIS | Très bien merci et vous? |
| M. LAYEN | Ça va merci. |

| 2 🎧 | DELAYING AN APPOINTMENT |
|---|---|

| | |
|---|---|
| M. LAYEN | Je regrette mais je ne peux pas venir lundi comme prévu. Est-ce qu'on pourrait remettre au lundi suivant? |
| M. NOBIS | Attendez . . . Ce n'est pas possible le lundi quatorze, je ne suis pas libre, mais le mercredi seize à quinze heures, ça va? |
| M. LAYEN | Tout à fait. Donc le mercredi seize à quinze heures, merci bien. |
| M. NOBIS | Mais je vous en prie. Au revoir Joseph. |
| M. LAYEN | Au revoir. |

## Greetings
*Comment allez-vous?*   How are you?
*(très) bien merci*   (very) well
*et vous?*   and you?

You will also hear the following forms of greeting, but they are only for people who know each other very well.
*(Comment) ça va?*   How are things?
*ça va*   fine

## Negatives
To say something is **not** so, you use *ne* and *pas* on each side of the verb:

*Je **ne** suis **pas** libre*   I am not free
*Je **ne** peux **pas***   I can't
*Ce **n'**est **pas** possible*   It is not possible
***Ne** quittez **pas***   Hold on (literally 'don't leave')

## Months (*les mois*)
As for the days, the months are all masculine and do not take a capital letter:

| | | | |
|---|---|---|---|
| *janvier* | January | *juillet* | July |
| *février* | February | *août* | August |
| *mars* | March | *septembre* | September |
| *avril* | April | *octobre* | October |
| *mai* | May | *novembre* | November |
| *juin* | June | *décembre* | December |

*en janvier*   in January
*en avril*   in April

## Dates
The date is always preceded by *le: le 4 janvier*.
Except for the first of the month, which is *le premier janvier*, use the normal numbers:

*le deux mars*   2 March
*le cinq juin*   5 June
*le vingt et un août*   21 August

🎧 **EXERCISE 2–3**
Listen to the dates and match them with the following:

**a** 2/12 **b** 1/5 **c** 12/7 **d** 20/2 **e** 31/8

You could also practise saying and writing them.

🎧 **EXERCISE 2–4**
Listen to conversation 2–3 again and answer the following questions:

**a** Which day does Mr Layen propose for the new appointment?
**b** Why is it not possible for Mr Nobis?
**c** Which date is convenient for Mr Nobis?
**d** At what time will the meeting take place?

## ● MEETING FOR THE FIRST TIME ●

| KEY WORDS AND PHRASES | |
|---|---|
| j'ai rendez-vous avec | I have an appointment with |
| veuillez patienter | could you please wait |
| je vais la prévenir | I'll let her know |
| enchanté | how do you do |
| votre voyage s'est bien passé? | did you have a good trip? |
| j'ai pris le TGV | I've come by high speed train |
| c'est rapide | it's fast |
| c'est pratique | it's handy |
| voici mon bureau | here is my office |
| asseyez-vous | do sit down |

## 2–4 Meeting for the first time

|  | I HAVE AN APPOINTMENT WITH |

| | |
|---|---|
| RÉCEPTIONNISTE | Bonjour monsieur. |
| M. LAYEN | Bonjour madame, je suis M. Layen. J'ai rendez-vous avec Mme Blois à onze heures. |
| RÉCEPTIONNISTE | Très bien monsieur, veuillez patienter, je vais la prévenir. |
| M. LAYEN | Merci madame. |

| 2 | HOW DO YOU DO? |

| | |
|---|---|
| MME BLOIS | Monsieur Layen? Je suis Monique Blois. Enchantée. |
| M. LAYEN | Enchanté madame. |

| 3 | HOW WAS YOUR JOURNEY? |

| | |
|---|---|
| MME BLOIS | Votre voyage s'est bien passé? |
| M. LAYEN | Très bien merci. J'ai pris le TGV, c'est rapide. |
| MME BLOIS | Oh oui, c'est très pratique. Voici mon bureau, asseyez-vous. |

## Asking people to do something

*veuillez patienter*   could you wait please
*patientez*   a moment please
*veuillez vous asseoir*   please sit down
*asseyez-vous*   do sit down
*je vous prie*   please

## Introductions

To introduce yourself use the expressions:

*Je suis Monique Blois*
*Je m'appelle Joseph Layen*

Once introduced, the French shake each other's hand and a man will say *enchanté* (*monsieur/madame*) ('how do you do') or *heureux de faire votre connaissance* ('pleased to meet you').

A woman will say *enchantée* (*monsieur/madame*) or *heureuse de faire votre connaissance*.

## Did you have a good journey?

*Votre voyage s'est bien passé?*
*Vous avez fait bon voyage?*

To answer:
(*très*) *bien merci*   (very) well thank you
*assez bien*   fairly well
*pas de problèmes*   no problems

## Describing the journey

*J'ai pris le TGV*   I travelled by high speed train
*c'est rapide*   it is fast
*c'est* (*très*) *pratique*   it is (very) handy

## EXERCISE 2–5

You are at the reception of your client's firm. Fill in your side of the conversation.

| | |
|---|---|
| RÉCEPTIONNISTE | Bonjour monsieur. |
| YOU | *Greet her and say you have an appointment with madame Delmas.* |
| RÉCEPTIONNISTE | C'est de la part de qui? |
| YOU | *Tell her your name and company.* |
| RÉCEPTIONNISTE | Bien monsieur, veuillez vous asseoir, je vais la prévenir. |
| YOU | *Thank her.* |
| MME DELMAS | Monsieur Sandell? Je suis Marielle Delmas, enchantée. |
| YOU | *Pleased to meet you.* |
| MME DELMAS | Vous avez fait bon voyage? |
| YOU | *Tell her you have not had any problems.* |
| MME DELMAS | Voici mon bureau. Asseyez–vous je vous prie. |
| YOU | *Thank her.* |

# ● TALKING ABOUT YOUR JOB/ COMPANY ●

| KEY WORDS AND PHRASES | |
|---|---|
| **voici ma carte de visite** | here is my card |
| **je suis responsable** | I am in charge |
| **des ventes pour l'Europe** | of sales throughout Europe |
| **notre siège social** | our head office |
| **est à Londres** | is in London |
| **nous fabriquons** | we manufacture/produce |
| **des pièces (de rechange)** | (spare) parts |
| **des accessoires** | accessories |
| **pour l'industrie automobile** | for the car industry |

## 2–5 I am the sales manager

| | INTRODUCING YOURSELF |
|---|---|

M. LAYEN — Je suis le chef des ventes de la compagnie
Norma. Voici ma carte de visite.

MME BLOIS — Merci.

M. LAYEN — Je suis responsable des ventes pour l'Europe.
Notre siège social est à Londres, nous
fabriquons des accessoires et des pièces de
rechange pour l'industrie automobile.

| EXPLANATIONS AND EXERCISES |
|---|

**Talking about your job**
To describe your job you can say:

*Je suis responsable des ventes pour l'Europe*
*Je suis chargé des ventes en Europe*

**To talk about your company**
When speaking about your company use:

*notre société*   our company
*notre siège social*   our head office
*nos produits*   our products
*nous fabriquons*   we manufacture
*nous vendons*   we sell
*nous offrons*   we offer

**Talking about towns and countries**
To say where you live or where you work or where your
company is located, use *à* in front of the name of the town:

*à Londres*   in London
*à Paris*   in Paris
*à Lyon*   in Lyon

But for a country, use *en* in front of a feminine country, *au*
for a masculine country and *aux* for a plural country:

**Feminine countries**

| | |
|---|---|
| *je représente* **la** *France* | *je travaille* **en** *France* |
| I am the representative for France | I work in France |
| *je représente* **l'***Angleterre* (England) | *je travaille* **en** *Angleterre* |
| *je représente* **l'***Allemagne* (Germany) | *je travaille* **en** *Allemagne* |

**Masculine countries**

| | |
|---|---|
| *je représente* **le** *Danemark* (Denmark) | *je travaille* **au** *Danemark* |
| *je représente* **le** *Japon* (Japan) | *je travaille* **au** *Japon* |

**Plural countries**

| | |
|---|---|
| *je représente* **les** *Etats-Unis* (United States of America) | *je travaille* **aux** *Etats-Unis* |
| *je représente* **les** *Pays-Bas* (Holland) | *je travaille* **aux** *Pays-Bas* |

**EXERCISE 2–6**
You tell the head buyer that your head office is in the suggested towns or countries below:

EXAMPLE    Madrid    Notre siège social est à Madrid en Espagne

| | | | | |
|---|---|---|---|---|
| **a** | Londres | | **d** | Tokyo |
| **b** | New-York | | **e** | Berlin |
| **c** | Paris | | | |

---

## WORTH KNOWING

**Formality and forms of address:**
French society is still very formal. There are certain rules that have to be followed, especially if you want to be taken seriously by French business colleagues.

When you meet people, and each time you meet them, **you must shake hands**. The same applies when you leave.

You must also say *bonjour* or *bonsoir* followed by *monsieur* or *madame*. Avoid using *mademoiselle*, which is only for young unmarried women. You won't be on first name terms for some time.

## Business organisation and structure

Here is a French company's typical structure:

| | |
|---|---|
| **Cadres supérieurs** Top management | *Président Directeur Général (PDG)* (MD) *Directeurs* (Directors) *Directeurs adjoints/Sous-directeurs* (Associate Directors) |
| **Cadres moyens** Middle management | *Chefs de services* — *production, technique, achats, ventes, après-ventes* (after-sales) *Sous-chefs de services* — *comptabilité* (accountancy) *contentieux* (legal) *personnel entretien* (maintenance) *Ingénieurs* (management engineers) *Techniciens supérieurs* (engineers) |
| **Cadres subalternes** Lower management | *Chefs de bureau* (head clerks) *Chefs d'atelier* (shop foremen) *Contremaîtres* (foremen) |
| **Employés** Office staff | *Sécretaires, Sténodactylos* (shorthand typists) *Représentants* (sales representatives) *Techniciens* (lower engineers) |
| **Main d'œuvre** Production staff | *Ouvriers qualifiés* (skilled workers) *Ouvriers spécialisés* (semi-skilled workers) *Manœuvres* (unskilled workers) |

Within the business organisation, the French are much more aware of hierarchy than the British or Americans. The post makes the person and confers on him or her

status and authority in the eyes of his or her colleagues and subordinates. This is reflected in their attitude, for example in the hand shake the more senior person will put his or her hand out first.

## SELF-ASSESSMENT

|  | I can | from memory (A) | with some reference to the text (B) | with full support (C) |
|---|---|---|---|---|
| on the phone | get through to the right person | | | |
| | introduce myself | | | |
| | make an appointment | | | |
| | change an appointment | | | |
| in person | ask for someone | | | |
| | introduce myself | | | |
| | say what my job is | | | |
| | talk about my firm | | | |

# 3 ENQUIRIES

## ● TASK ●

This unit will take you from making enquiries about product ranges, prices and stock availability to discussing sales terms and conditions with a view to placing an order.

## ● TALKING ABOUT PRODUCT RANGE ●

| KEY WORDS AND PHRASES | |
|---|---|
| **alors** | so/then |
| **pour** | for |
| **l'industrie automobile** | the car industry |
| **un catalogue/une brochure** | a catalogue/a brochure |
| **notre dernier catalogue** | our last catalogue |
| **avec** | with |
| **la gamme** | the range |
| **notre gamme complète** | our complete range |
| **tous vos produits** | all your products |
| **sont garantis** | are guaranteed |
| **naturellement** | naturally/of course |
| **un an** | one year |

# 3–1 Enquiring about product range

## SO YOU MAKE SPARE PARTS?

MME BLOIS   Alors vous fabriquez des pièces de rechange pour l'industrie automobile?

M. LAYEN   C'est ça, des pièces de rechange et des accessoires. Voici notre dernier catalogue avec notre gamme complète.

MME BLOIS   Tous vos produits sont garantis?

M. LAYEN   Naturellement, tous nos produits sont garantis un an.

## EXPLANATIONS AND EXERCISES

**Products and product range**
*les pièces de rechange*   spare parts
*la pièce (détachée)*   (spare) part
*le catalogue*   catalogue
*la brochure*   brochure
*la gamme complète*   the (complete) range

**Possessive adjectives: 'my', 'our', 'your'**
As with *le*, *la* and *les*, possessive adjectives vary with the gender of the possessed thing:

My

|  | **Masc.** (*le*) | **Fem.** (*la*) | **Plural** (*les*) |
|---|---|---|---|
| my | *mon* | *ma* | *mes* |

It makes no difference whether you are a man or a woman. You say:
*mon ticket*   my ticket
*ma société*   my company
*mes produits*   my products

Our

|  | **Masc.** (*le*) | **Fem.** (*la*) | **Plural** (*les*) |
|---|---|---|---|
| our | *notre* | *notre* | *nos* |

You say:
*notre ticket*   our ticket
*notre société*   our company
*nos produits*   our products

Your

|  | **Masc.** (*le*) | **Fem.** (*la*) | **Plural** (*les*) |
|---|---|---|---|
| your | *votre* | *votre* | *vos* |

You say:
*votre ticket*   your ticket
*votre société*   your company
*vos produits*   your products

**EXERCISE 3–1**

You are giving someone the following objects, which all belong to you:

EXAMPLE:   les bagages: Voici mes bagages

**a**   le billet
**b**   la carte de visite
**c**   le catalogue
**d**   les produits

Now you are serving a customer. You give him or her the following things:

EXAMPLE:   le produit: Voici votre produit

**e**   la clé
**f**   les pièces de rechange
**g**   le petit-déjeuner

Now you work for a large company and you are
introducing your product range using 'our':

EXAMPLE:    la brochure: Voici notre brochure,

**h**  le catalogue
**i**   les produits
**j**   la gamme complète

### Verbs

When speaking to other people you need to use 'you' (*vous*)
and 'I' (*je*). If you work for a large company you will also
use 'we' (*nous*). In French, verb endings change a lot more
than in English.

With *vous* most verbs end with -*ez*:

*vous **prenez***    you take
*vous **allez***    you go
*vous **fabriquez***    you manufacture
*ne **quittez** pas*    hold on
***asseyez**-vous*    sit down

With *nous* almost all verbs end with *-ons*:

*nous **fabriquons*** we produce
*nous **vendons*** we sell
*nous **offrons*** we offer

But with *je*, the endings vary:

*je **suis*** I am
*je **voudrais*** I would like
*j'**ai*** I have
*je vous en **prie*** please do

In fact the majority of verbs follow certain patterns. They are classified in three groups. The largest group is the *-er* group, *er* because when they are in the form 'to __', they end with *-er* (*fabriquer* 'to make', *présenter* 'to present, introduce', *s'appeler* 'to be called').

In grammar books or dictionaries, verb tables are always presented in the same order.

Most verbs ending in *-er* are formed as follows:

|  |  |
|---|---|
| **fabriquer** to produce | |
| **je** *fabrique* I produce/I am producing | **nous** *fabriquons* we produce/are producing |
| **tu** *fabriques* you produce/are producing | **vous** *fabriquez* you produce/are producing |
| **il/elle** *fabrique* he/she produces/is producing | **ils/elles** *fabriquent* they produce/are producing |

|  |  |
|---|---|
| **travailler** to work | |
| **je** *travaille* I work | **nous** *travaillons* we work |
| **tu** *travailles* you work | **vous** *travaillez* you work |
| **il/elle** *travaille* he/she works | **ils/elles** *travaillent* they work |

The English form 'I am producing' does not exist in French. Use the equivalent of 'I produce', *je fabrique*.

*Vous fabriquez des pièces de rechange*    you are producing spare parts

'You' is *tu* when you speak to relatives, children and close friends.

For business you should always use *vous* unless invited to use *tu*.

Unfortunately some verbs do not follow the normal pattern. Two very important irregular verbs are:

|  | *être*   to be |  |
|---|---|---|
| *je suis*   I am | | *nous sommes*   we are |
| *tu es*   you are | | *vous êtes*   you are |
| *il/elle est*   he/she is | | *ils/elles sont*   they are |

|  | *avoir*   to have |  |
|---|---|---|
| *j'ai*   I have | | *nous avons*   we have |
| *tu as*   you have | | *vous avez*   you have |
| *il/elle a*   he/she has | | *ils/elles ont*   they have |

## EXERCISE 3–2

A prospective customer wants to know about your company and your products. Answer his questions using *nous*.

EXAMPLE    Client   Alors vous fabriquez des pièces de rechange?

Vous   C'est ça, nous fabriquons des pièces de rechange.

**a**   Alors vous vendez des pièces de rechange?
**b**   Alors vous avez un catalogue?
**c**   Alors vous garantissez vos produits?
**d**   Alors vous offrez la gamme complète?
**e**   Alors vous travaillez en France?

# • ASKING ABOUT PRICES •

### KEY WORDS AND PHRASES

| | |
|---|---|
| **le prix** | price |
| **le tarif** | price list/rate |
| **la liste des prix** | price list |
| **c'est** | it is |
| **(prix) franco domicile** | free delivery |
| **(prix) sortie d'usine** | ex-works/factory (price) |
| **et bien** | well |
| **je vais regarder** | I am going to look at |
| **tout ça** | all that |
| **je vous rappellerai** | I'll call you back |

## 3–2 Asking about prices

### HOW ABOUT PRICES?

| | |
|---|---|
| MME BLOIS | Et vos prix? |
| M. LAYEN | Voici nos tarifs. |
| MME BLOIS | C'est la liste des prix franco domicile? |
| M. LAYEN | Ah non. Sortie d'usine. |
| MME BLOIS | Et bien, je vais regarder tout ça et je vous rappellerai. |

### EXPLANATIONS AND EXERCISES

**Price and transport**
The French terminology for transport costs is very similar to English:

| | | | |
|---|---|---|---|
| *prix FOB* | FOB price | *prix sortie d'usine* | factory price |
| *prix CAF* | CIF price | *prix franco domicile* | free delivery |
| *prix CF* | CF price | *une assurance* | insurance |
| | | *le tarif/la liste des prix* | price list |

## Spelling and the alphabet

To ask someone to spell their name, just say:

*Pouvez-vous épeler votre nom?* can you spell your name?

Spelling foreign names or saying abbreviated words like *FOB* or even quoting reference numbers is often necessary in business. The French alphabet has the same letters as the English one, but the pronunciation is different.

Learn and practise saying the French alphabet with the recording. The pronunciation guide will also give you some ideas about vowels and nasal sounds.

Accents are very important in French because not only do they usually change the pronunciation of the vowel, but also the meaning of the word. For example *mais* pronounced as a short 'May' means 'but', whereas *maïs* means 'corn/maize' and is pronounced as 'ma' in 'map' followed by 'iss' in 'miss', 'ma–iss'. In the same way *la tache* means 'stain' but *la tâche* means 'duty'.

### 🎧 EXERCISE 3–3

Listen to the spellings and match them with the following:

**a** TGV **b** RER **c** CAF **d** FOB **e** EDFGDF

## I am going to

To say what you are going to do later on or on the following day or in the near future, just use the verb *aller*, 'to go', followed by the 'to __' form of the verb. (The 'to __' form is called the infinitive.)

*je vais regarder* I am going to look at
*nous allons fabriquer* we are going to manufacture
*vous allez vendre* you are going to sell

*Aller* is another irregular verb (see overleaf).

| *aller* to go | | | |
|---|---|---|---|
| *je vais* | I am going/I go | *nous allons* | we are going/go |
| *tu vas* | you are going/you go | *vous allez* | you are going/go |
| *il/elle va* | he/she is going/goes | *ils/elles vont* | they are going/go |

**EXERCISE 3–4**

Say you are going to do the following tomorrow, *demain*:

EXAMPLE    Vous prenez le train aujourd'hui?
Non mais je vais prendre le train demain.

**a**   Vous êtes libre aujourd'hui?
**b**   Vous avez un rendez-vous aujourd'hui?
**c**   Vous regardez le catalogue aujourd'hui?
**d**   Vous réservez une chambre aujourd'hui?

# ● ENQUIRING ABOUT STOCK AVAILABILITY ●

## KEY WORDS AND PHRASES

| | |
|---|---|
| **la pièce** | part |
| **référence (réf.)** | reference |
| **en stock** | in stock |
| **en magasin** | in stock/warehouse |
| **pourriez-vous?** | could you? |
| **mettre** | to put |
| **la commande** | order |
| **quel est le numéro?** | what is the number? |
| **c'est noté** | I've made a note of it |
| **confirmer** | to confirm |
| **par télex/fax** | by telex/fax |
| **à votre service** | at your service/you're welcome |
| **un fournisseur** | supplier |

## 3–3 Enquiring about stock availability

DO YOU HAVE PART NUMBER 352 IN STOCK?

| | |
|---|---|
| FOURNISSEUR | Allô, ici la société Duros. |
| CLIENTE | Bonjour, ici les Etablissements Bourgeois. Avez-vous les pièces réf. AD 352 en stock? |
| FOURNISSEUR | Référence AD 352. Patientez un moment s'il vous plaît. . . . Allô? oui, nous en avons dix en magasin. |
| CLIENTE | Ah très bien. Pourriez-vous en mettre quatre avec notre commande du six juin? |
| FOURNISSEUR | Bien sûr madame. Avez-vous le numéro de la commande? |
| CLIENTE | Numéro 458. |
| FOURNISSEUR | C'est noté. Pourriez-vous confirmer par télex? |
| CLIENTE | D'accord. Au revoir et merci bien. |
| FOURNISSEUR | A votre service. Au revoir madame. |

## Asking questions

The simplest way of asking a question is to use a statement with a rising intonation at the end:

*Vous fabriquez des pièces de rechange?*
*Vous avez les pièces réf. AD 352 en stock?*

You can also start with *est-ce que* in front of the statement:

**Est-ce que** *vous fabriquez des pièces de rechange?*
**Est-ce que** *vous avez les pièces réf. AD 352 en stock?*

Some questions begin with a verb:

**Fabriquez**-*vous des pièces de rechange?*
**Avez**-*vous les pièces réf. AD 352 en stock?*
**Avez**-*vous le numéro de la commande?*

Finally, questions can begin with a question word:

**Quand** *puis-je la joindre?*    When can I reach her?
*A* **quelle** *heure servez-vous le petit-déjeuner?*    At what time do you serve breakfast?
**Quel** *train?*    Which train?
**Où** *est la sortie?*    Where is the exit?

## Talking about a number of articles you have already mentioned

*Avez vous les pièces AD 352 en stock?*
*Nous* **en** *avons* **dix**    We have **ten of them**
*Pourriez-vous* **en** *mettre* **quatre** . . . ?    Could you put **four of them** . . . ?

🎧    **EXERCISE 3–5**

Listen to conversation 3–3 again to find out:

**a**    Which parts is the customer asking about?
**b**    How many of them has the supplier got in stock?
**c**    How many does the customer want?
**d**    What is the date and the number of the order?
**e**    How is the customer going to confirm the order?

# ● MORE ABOUT PRICES AND LEAD TIMES ●

| KEY WORDS AND PHRASES | |
| --- | --- |
| m'intéressent | interest me/I am interested in |
| lesquels | which ones |
| en effet | actually |
| ces articles | these items/articles |
| ont beaucoup de succès | have a lot of success |
| c'est pour quelle quantité? | which quantity is it for? |
| ce sont | they are |
| les prix unitaires | unit prices |
| il y a | there is/there are |
| une remise de 5% | a 5% discount |
| disons | let us say |
| supérieure à | greater than |
| les délais de livraison | lead time/delivery time |
| quinze jours | a fortnight |

## 3–4 Finding out more about prices and lead times

| WHEN WILL YOU DELIVER? | |
| --- | --- |
| MME BLOIS | Deux pièces de rechange m'intéressent. |
| M. LAYEN | Ah oui, lesquels? |
| MME BLOIS | Les articles référence DB 120 et CF 435. |
| M. LAYEN | En effet ces articles ont beaucoup de succès. |
| MME BLOIS | Les prix? C'est pour quelle quantité? |
| M. LAYEN | Ce sont les prix unitaires. Pour une commande de cinquante pièces il y a une remise de 5%, et 9% pour cent pièces. |
| MME BLOIS | Et pour une première commande? |

| M. LAYEN | Disons . . . 2% pour une commande supérieure à cinquante pièces. |
| MME BLOIS | Et les délais de livraison? |
| M. LAYEN | Quinze jours. |

### EXPLANATIONS AND EXERCISES

## Showing interest and describing things
*deux pièces de rechange m'intéressent*    I am interested in two spare parts
*j'aime*    I like
*lesquels*    which ones
*en effet*    an expression which introduces an explanation
*ces articles ont beaucoup de succès*    these items have a lot of success
*ces articles se vendent bien*    these items sell well

## C'est, ce sont . . . 'it is', 'they are'
When pointing to or referring to something which is not named, use *c'est* for a single thing or idea and *ce sont* for more than one thing.

*c'est pour quelle quantité?*    which quantity is it for?
*c'est ça*    that is right
*c'est noté*    (it is noted) I have noted it down
*ce sont les prix unitaires*    they are unit prices

## Describing the order
*une commande de 50 pièces*    an order for 50 items
*une première commande*    a first order
*une commande supérieure à*    an order greater than

## Terms and conditions
*une remise*    a discount/reduction
*une escompte*    a discount
*un rabais (une réduction)*    a reduction
*une remise **de** neuf pour cent*    a 9% discount
*les délais de livraison*    lead time/delivery time
*quinze jours*    a fortnight

🎧 **EXERCISE 3–6**

Listen to the discounts offered and match them with the following:

**a** 8% pour une commande supérieure à 30 pièces
**b** 2% pour une commande supérieure à 5000F
**c** 6% pour une commande de 75 pièces
**d** 3% pour la première commande
**e** 7% à partir de cent pièces

🎧 **EXERCISE 3–7**

Listen to conversation 3–4 to find out:

**a** Which items is madame Blois interested in?
**b** Which quantity must she order to get a 5% discount and to get a 9% discount?
**c** What does the 2% refer to?
**d** What is the delivery time?

# ● PLACING AN ORDER ●

| KEY WORDS AND PHRASES | |
|---|---|
| **donc** | so |
| **compter sur** | to count on/to rely on |
| **la livraison** | delivery |
| **dans quinze jours** | in a fortnight |
| **envoyer** | to send |
| **je vous envoie** | I am sending you |
| **le bon de commande** | order form |
| **immédiatement** | immediately |

## 3–5 Placing an order

🎧          I'D LIKE . . .

| | |
|---|---|
| MME BLOIS | Alors je voudrais vingt-cinq accessoires référence DB 120 et vingt-cinq référence CF 435. |
| M. LAYEN | Très bien. C'est noté. |
| MME BLOIS | Merci. Donc nous comptons sur la livraison dans quinze jours. |
| M. LAYEN | C'est ça. Euh, pourriez-vous confirmer la commande? |
| MME BLOIS | D'accord. Je vous envoie le bon de commande immédiatement. |
| M. LAYEN | Merci beaucoup. Au revoir madame Blois. |
| MME BLOIS | Au revoir monsieur Layen. |

### EXPLANATIONS AND EXERCISES

**More dates**

To say something is going to happen in a fortnight or in a week use *dans* followed by the length of time:

*dans trois jours*    in three days' time
*dans une semaine*    in a week's time
*dans quinze jours*    in a fortnight
*dans un mois*    in a month's time
*dans un an*    in a year's time
*aujourd'hui*    today
*maintenant*    now
*immédiatement*    immediately

🎧    **EXERCISE 3–8**

Listen to the dates being read out and match them with the following:

**a**   5 jours   **b**   48 heures   **c**   3 semaines   **d**   demain

**e**   1 mois

## EXERCISE 3–9

How would you say in French:

**a** I would like 20 spare parts reference TR 156.
**b** We will expect (rely on) delivery in a fortnight.
**c** I'll send you the order form straight away.

---

### WORTH KNOWING

---

**Types of companies:**

There are three main types of companies.

*1 La Société à Responsabilité Limitée, SARL*
This is the most common type in France as it is suitable for most small businesses. It must have at least two shareholders and at most fifty, with a minimum share capital of 50 000 francs. The shares are only transferable amongst the existing shareholders. The company is run by one or several managers (*gérants*) and has no board of directors.

*2 L'Entreprise Unipersonnelle à Responsabilité Limitée, EURL*
Since 1985, an individual can form a EURL. This is most attractive to small foreign companies since it only needs to have one share and thus keeps control over all decisions.

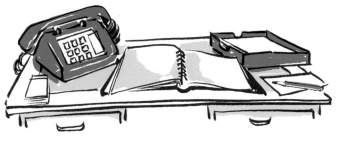

### 3   La Société Anonyme, SA

This is a public company, similar to the British plc. It has to have a minimum of seven shareholders (*actionnaires*) and 250 000 francs of share capital (*capital social*) if not quoted on the stock exchange (*la Bourse*) or 1.5m if quoted (*cotée*). It is run by a *President Directeur Général* (*PDG*) who is appointed by a board of directors (*le conseil d'administration*).

**Where to find information:** *Chambres de Commerce et d'Industrie* (*CCI*)
If you need information about firms, contact the local chambers of commerce, which constantly try to promote and develop their region and have a much more comprehensive role than their British counterparts.

They have a record of all the activities going on in their region because all companies must register with them before starting business. They conduct a lot of vocational training financed by *la taxe d'apprentissage* (a training tax), which must be paid by all companies. Finally they are responsible for the running of all regional ports and airports.

| SELF-ASSESSMENT | | | |
|---|---|---|---|
| **I can** | **from memory (A)** | **with some reference to the text (B)** | **with full support (C)** |
| introduce my products | | | |
| enquire about range | | | |
| enquire about product availability | | | |
| discuss terms and prices | | | |
| place an order | | | |

# 4 BUSINESS PROBLEMS

## ● TASK ●

This unit will help you to complain about a problem to a supplier as well as dealing with a complaint from a customer. The problems dealt with are faulty products, late deliveries and unsettled bills.

## ● A COMPLAINT ABOUT FAULTY PRODUCTS ●

| KEY WORDS AND PHRASES | |
|---|---|
| **un problème** | a problem |
| **Qu'est-ce qui ne va pas?** | what's wrong? |
| **les batteries** | batteries |
| **ne marchent pas** | do not work |
| **elles ne restent pas** | they do not stay |
| **chargées** | charged |
| **je vais me renseigner** | I am going to enquire/ find out |
| **la dernière livraison** | the last delivery |

## 4–1 We have a problem with . . .

| | THE BATTERIES DON'T WORK |
|---|---|

| | |
|---|---|
| STANDARDISTE | Ici la compagnie Norma. |
| M. AHMED | Je voudrais parler à monsieur Layen s'il vous plaît. |
| STANDARDISTE | Ne quittez pas, je vous le passe . . . |
| M. LAYEN | Joseph Layen à l'appareil. |
| M. AHMED | Bonjour, ici Abdul Ahmed. Comment allez-vous? |
| M. LAYEN | Très bien merci et vous? |
| M. AHMED | Ça va. Mais j'ai un problème avec votre dernière livraison. |
| M. LAYEN | Qu'est-ce qui ne va pas? |
| M. AHMED | Et bien, les batteries ne marchent pas bien. Elles ne restent pas chargées. |
| M. LAYEN | Quelles batteries? |
| M. AHMED | V12. |
| M. LAYEN | Bon, je vais me renseigner et je vous rappellerai. |
| M. AHMED | D'accord, merci. |

| EXPLANATIONS AND EXERCISES |
|---|

### Stating the problem

*J'ai un problème*   I have a problem
*Les batteries ne marchent pas bien*   The batteries don't work well
*Le téléphone ne marche pas*   The phone does not work
*La machine est en panne*   The machine is out of order
*Elles ne restent pas chargées*   They don't stay charged (keep their charge)

Or it could be:

*Ce n'est pas le bon article*   It is not the right article
*Ce n'est pas la bonne qualité*   It is not the right quality
*C'est le mauvais article*   It is the wrong article
*C'est la mauvaise taille*   It is the wrong size

*Les articles sont cassés*   The items are broken
*L'emballage est endommagé*   The packaging is damaged

## Asking about the problem
*Qu'est-ce qui ne va pas?*   What's wrong?
*Quel est le problème?*   What's the problem?

## 'Me', 'you'
To tell people you are doing or are going to do something
for them you say:

*Je **vous** rappellerai*   I will call **you** back
*Pour **vous** présenter*   to show **you**
*Je **vous** envoie*   I am sending **you**

To ask people to do something for you, say:

*Pourriez-vous **me** réveiller?*   Could you wake **me** up?

*Me* is also frequently used for 'myself':

*Je m'appelle*   (literally: 'I call myself') My name is
*Je me renseigne*   I am making enquiries (myself)

These last two verbs are called reflexive verbs and are
conjugated (formed) as follows:

|  *s'appeler*   to be called | | | |
|---|---|---|---|
| **je m'**appelle | I am called | **nous nous** appelons | we are called |
| **tu t'**appelles | you are called | **vous vous** appelez | you are called |
| **il/elle s'**appelle | he/she is called | **ils/elles s'**appellent | they are called |

|  *se renseigner*   to enquire | | | |
|---|---|---|---|
| **je me** renseigne | I enquire | **nous nous** renseignons | we enquire |
| **tu te** renseignes | you enquire | **vous vous** renseignez | you enquire |
| **il/elle se** renseigne | he/she enquires | **ils/elles se** renseignent | they enquire |

Often the same verb can be used as reflexive and non-
reflexive:

*je m'appelle*   means 'I am called' or 'I call myself'
*j'appelle*   means 'I call'

When non-reflexive, *renseigner* means 'to give information' (*je renseigne* 'I give information'). But *se renseigner* is 'to get information' (*je me renseigne* 'I get information' or 'I enquire').

*le bureau des renseignements*   information desk/office.

**EXERCISE 4–1**
How would you say:

a   My name is Pierre.
b   I am going to make enquiries.
c   I'll call you back.
d   I would like to present our products to you.
e   Could you wake me up at 7 am?

**EXERCISE 4–2**
Could you complain about the following problems?

a   The phone does not work.
b   The machine is out of order.
c   It's the wrong size.
d   It's not the right quality.

## ● SOLVING THE PROBLEM ●

| KEY WORDS AND PHRASES | |
|---|---|
| **nous avons trouvé** | we have found |
| **nous allons changer** | we are going to change |
| **pas plus tard** | not later |
| **nos clients les attendent** | our customers are waiting for them |
| **je vous prie de** | please (literally 'I pray you to') |
| **nous excuser** | excuse us |
| **une erreur de production** | a manufacturing error/mistake |

## 4–2 We have solved the problem

### 🎧 WE'LL CHANGE THE BATTERIES

| | |
|---|---|
| M. LAYEN | Nous avons trouvé le problème et nous allons changer les batteries. |
| M. AHMED | Ah merci! Quand? |
| M. LAYEN | La semaine prochaine. |
| M. AHMED | D'accord, mais pas plus tard, nos clients les attendent. |
| M. LAYEN | Je vous prie de nous excuser. C'est une erreur de production et . . . |

### EXPLANATIONS AND EXERCISES

**We have found**

To form the past (perfect) tense use *avoir*, 'to have', followed by the verb in its past participle form, for example, 'found', *trouvé*.

|  | *trouver* (perfect tense) | | |
|---|---|---|---|
| **j'ai** trouvé | I have found | **nous avons** trouvé | we have found |
| **tu as** trouvé | you have found | **vous avez** trouvé | you have found |
| **il/elle a** trouvé | he/she has found | **ils/elles ont** trouvé | they have found |

The past participle of -*er* verbs is formed by replacing the -*er* by -*é*. This does not change the pronunciation.

*changer* becomes *j'ai changé*, 'I have changed'
*parler* becomes *j'ai parlé*, 'I have spoken'
*confirmer* becomes *nous avons confirmé*, 'we have confirmed'
*envoyer* becomes *vous avez envoyé*, 'you have sent'

There are some other forms of past participles:

*prendre* becomes *j'ai **pris***, 'I have taken'
*garantir* becomes *j'ai garanti*, 'I have guaranteed'
*vendre* becomes *nous avons vend**u***, 'we have sold'

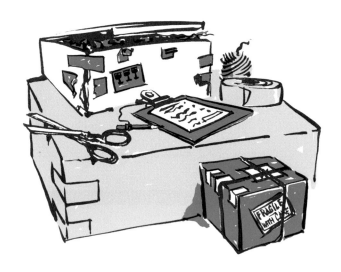

**EXERCISE 4–3**

You are asked to do the following things and you answer
that you did them yesterday, *hier.*

EXAMPLE    Pourriez-vous envoyer la commande?
                    Mais j'ai envoyé la commande hier.

**a**  Pourriez-vous confirmer la commande?
**b**  Pourriez-vous réserver une chambre d'hôtel?
**c**  Pourriez-vous regarder notre catalogue?
**d**  Pourriez-vous prendre le train?
**e**  Pourriez-vous parler au PDG?

**Late, later . . .**
*tard*   late
*Il est tard*   It is late (in the day)
*trop tard*   too late
*pas plus tard*   not later
*en retard*   late
*Il est en retard*   He is late (for an appointment)

*tôt*   early
*Il est tôt*   It is early (in the day)
*en avance*   early
*Il est en avance*   he is early (for an appointment)

**I am sorry**
We have already encountered two simple ways of apologising: *malheureusement* and *je regrette*.

You could also use:

*Je suis (vraiment) désolé*   I am (really) sorry

But if you really want a customer to forgive a mistake made by your company, use (in ascending order of formality):

*Excusez-nous*   Excuse us
*Je vous prie de nous excuser*   Please excuse us
*Veuillez nous excuser*   Please excuse us

Some useful expressions are:

*Je ne sais pas*   I don't know
*Je ne savais pas*   I didn't know
*Je ne comprends pas*   I don't understand
*Je vais me renseigner*   I am going to find out
*C'est une erreur*   It's a mistake
*Ce n'est pas de notre faute*   It's not our fault
*C'est la faute du transporteur*   It's the carrier's fault.

**EXERCISE 4–4**
How would you say:

**a**   I am sorry, I am late.
**b**   Please excuse us, it's a mistake.
**c**   Unfortunately, it is too late.
**d**   I am very sorry, I am going to find out.

# ● I AM STILL WAITING! ●

| KEY WORDS AND PHRASES | |
|---|---|
| **laisser un message** | leave a message |
| **j'attends toujours** | I'm still waiting |
| **le numéro de téléphone** | phone number |
| **dès que possible** | as soon as possible |
| **dites-lui** | tell him |
| **que** | that |
| **c'est urgent** | it's urgent |

## 4–3 We are still waiting for delivery

| 🎧 | IT'S URGENT |
|---|---|

| | |
|---|---|
| SECRÉTAIRE | Allô, ici le service des ventes. |
| M. AHMED | Je voudrais parler à monsieur Layen s'il vous plaît. |
| SECRÉTAIRE | Monsieur Layen est en conférence. Voulez-vous laisser un message? |
| M. AHMED | Oui merci. J'attends toujours la livraison des batteries V12. |
| SECRÉTAIRE | Et vous êtes monsieur? |
| M. AHMED | Abdul Ahmed. |
| SECRÉTAIRE | Et votre numéro de téléphone M. Ahmed? |
| M. AHMED | C'est le 31 53 75 20. |
| SECRÉTAIRE | M. Layen vous rappellera dès que possible. |
| M. AHMED | Dites-lui bien que c'est urgent. |
| SECRÉTAIRE | D'accord, au revoir M. Ahmed. |
| M. AHMED | Au revoir madame. |

## EXPLANATIONS AND EXERCISES

### Leaving a message

To offer to take a message you can use:

*Voulez-vous laisser un message?*   Would you like to leave a message?
*Puis-je prendre un message?*   May I take a message?
*Je pourrais lui donner un message*   I could give him/her a message

To ask to leave a message:

*Je voudrais laisser un message*   I would like to leave a message
*Est-ce que je pourrais laisser un message?*   Could I leave a message?
*Puis-je laisser un message?*   May I leave a message?

| *Pourriez-vous* | Could you |
| --- | --- |
| *prendre un message?* | take a message? |
| *lui donner un message?* | give him/her a message? |
| *lui dire de* | tell him/her to |

*Dites-lui que*   Tell him/her that

### More numbers

| 60 soixante | 61 soixante et un |
| --- | --- |
| 62 soixante-deux | 63 soixante-trois |
| 70 soixante-dix | 71 soixante et onze |
| 72 soixante-douze | 73 soixante-treize |
| 80 quatre-vingts | 81 quatre-vingt-un |
| 82 quatre-vingt-deux | 83 quatre-vingt-trois |
| 90 quatre-vingt-dix | 91 quatre-vingt-onze |
| 92 quatre-vingt-douze | 93 quatre-vingt-treize |

Up to 71, there is *et* in between the ten and the unit, *vingt et un, trente et un, soixante et un, soixante et onze*, but it is not there for either *quatre-vingt-un* or for *quatre-vingt-onze*.

## Telephone numbers
French telephone numbers have eight digits and are said in pairs.

## What's your phone number?
To ask for someone's phone number or address:

*Quel est votre numéro de téléphone?*　What's your phone number?
*Quelle est votre adresse?*　What's your address?

You may also be asked: *quelles sont vos coordonnées?* for both your address and telephone number.

🎧　EXERCISE 4–5
Listen to the phone numbers and match them with the following:

| | | | | |
|---|---|---|---|---|
| **a** | 45 38 01 34 | | **d** | 20 17 73 63 |
| **b** | 12 50 21 60 | | **e** | 31 09 86 27 |
| **c** | 12 15 92 02 | | **f** | 65 43 78 10 |

## Who's speaking?
To ask who is on the other end of the phone:

*Vous êtes monsieur/madame?*
*Quel est votre nom?*　What's your name?
*Puis-je avoir votre nom?*　May I have your name?
*Qui est à l'appareil?*　Who is on the phone?
*C'est de la part de qui?*　Who is it from? (literally, 'on whose behalf')

**EXERCISE 4–6**
Could you leave a message? Fill in your side of the
conversation.

| | |
|---|---|
| SECRÉTAIRE | Allô, ici le service des ventes. |
| YOU | *Ask to speak to monsieur Platini.* |
| SECRÉTAIRE | Je regrette mais monsieur Platini est en conférence. |
| YOU | *Ask when you could contact him.* |
| SECRÉTAIRE | Je ne sais pas exactement, voulez-vous laisser un message? |
| YOU | *Say yes, you are still waiting for the last delivery.* |
| SECRÉTAIRE | Quel est votre nom? |
| YOU | *Give her your name.* |
| SECRÉTAIRE | Quel est votre numéro de téléphone? |
| YOU | *Give her your number.* |
| SECRÉTAIRE | Monsieur Platini vous rappellera dès que possible. Au revoir monsieur. |
| YOU | *Say good bye.* |

## ● UNSETTLED BILLS ●

| KEY WORDS AND PHRASES | |
|---|---|
| **la comptabilité** | accountancy |
| **la facture** | the bill/invoice |
| **n'a pas été réglée** | has not been settled |
| **nous n'avons pas reçu** | we have not received |
| **les nouvelles batteries** | the new batteries |
| **je ne comprends pas** | I don't understand |
| **vous devez** | you must/you are supposed to |
| **remplacer** | replace |
| **je ne savais pas** | I didn't know |

## 4–4 The bill has not been settled

| 🎧 | I DIDN'T KNOW |
|---|---|

| | |
|---|---|
| EMPLOYÉE | Allô ici le service de la comptabilité. |
| FOURNISSEUR | Allô bonjour madame. Ici l'entreprise Norma. |
| | Notre facture du 16 mars n'a pas été réglée. |
| EMPLOYÉE | Avez-vous le numéro de la facture? |
| FOURNISSEUR | Oui, numéro 1230. |
| EMPLOYÉE | Patientez un moment s'il vous plaît . . . |
| | Voilà, j'ai trouvé la facture. Nous n'avons pas reçu les nouvelles batteries. |
| FOURNISSEUR | Je ne comprends pas . . . |
| EMPLOYÉE | Vous devez remplacer les batteries V12 et nous attendons toujours les nouvelles. |
| FOURNISSEUR | Ah excusez-moi, je ne savais pas . . . |

### EXPLANATIONS AND EXERCISES

**We have *not* received**

For the negative form of the perfect tense just add *ne* and *pas* on each side of *avoir* (*ne* becomes *n'* in front of a vowel).

*nous n'avons pas reçu*    we have not received

Compare and learn the affirmative and negative forms:

| affirmative | negative |
|---|---|
| j'ai pris | je n'ai pas pris |
| tu as parlé | tu n'as pas parlé |
| il/elle a envoyé | il/elle n'a pas envoyé |
| nous avons reçu | nous n'avons pas reçu |
| vous avez réglé | vous n'avez pas réglé |
| ils/elles ont attendu | ils/elles n'ont pas attendu |

Levallois, le 15 Juin 1990

J.B.C
135 RUE DU FG SAINT-HONOR
B.P. 407-06
75366 PARIS CEDEX 08

No Cde : F.11.C6.90
No bons: 92386/
Film No: 89C9558
FOURNITURE(S)                                    FACTURE No : 057139

| Quantité | Valeur unitaire | Désignation des travaux | Montant |
|---|---|---|---|
| 50 | 2C,00 | Rouleau de Scotch pour presse 16MM................ | 1.000,00 |
| 4 | 22,CC | Rouleau de scotch couleur........................ | 88,00 |
| 1C | 29,00 | Paire de Gants de Montage........................ | 290,00 |
| 5C | 8,25 | Noyaux TV en 16MM................................ | 412,50 |
| 7ECC | 1,13 | Amorce Bleue 16 MM............................... | 8.814,00 |
| 288C | C,74 | Amorce Blanche 16 MM............................. | 2.131,20 |
| | | | --------- |
| | | | 12.735,70 |
| | | T.V.A. 18,60 % | 2.368,84 |
| | | | --------- |
| | | Total  T.T.C. | 15.104,54 |

5, Place du Général Leclerc - B.P. 198
92300 Levallois-Perret Cédex
☎ 40.89.80.00 +
TÉLÉCOPIEUR : 47.48.04.87
TELEX : TELCIPR 614 267 F
s.a. au capital de 8.568.000 F
R.C.S. Nanterre B 311 068 829
SIRET 311 068 829 00028

En votre aimable règlement par Cheque a reception
(TVA acquittée sur les encaissements)
ATTENTION : Voir au verso extraits de nos conditions générales

TÉCTIS

## EXERCISE 4–7
Can you make the following statements negative?

**a**  J'ai réservé une chambre à deux lits.
**b**  Vous avez remplacé les articles.
**c**  Nous avons reçu la livraison.
**d**  Il m'a rappelé hier.
**e**  Elles ont envoyé la commande.
**f**  La facture a été réglée.
**g**  J'ai commandé ça.

## You must
*Vous devez* is a very useful verb to know when you want to remind people of their obligations (it has the double meaning 'you must' or 'you are supposed to/you have to'). It is irregular (see overleaf).

| devoir must (to have to) | | | |
|---|---|---|---|
| *je dois* | I must | *nous devons* | we must |
| *tu dois* | you must | *vous devez* | you must |
| *il/elle doit* | he/she must | *ils/elles doivent* | they must |

*vous devez remplacer*   you are supposed to replace
*vous devez rappeler le client*   you must call the client back
*vous devez régler la facture*   you must settle the bill

**WORTH KNOWING**

Telephoning
**To call a customer in France from Great Britain** dial 010 33 followed by

- 1 and the eight digit number if it is a Paris number
- the eight digit number for the rest of France (*la province*).

**To call a customer from France** you can buy a telephone card from the post office and most newsagents. After putting your card into the slot in a public phone, dial. There are three possibilities:

- within Paris or *la province*, dial the eight-figure number only
- from Paris to *la province*, dial 16, wait for the tone (*la tonalité*), then dial the eight-digit number
- from *la province* to Paris, dial 16, wait for the tone, then dial 1 followed by the eight–digit number

**To telephone Great Britain from France**, dial 19 and wait for the tone, then 44 followed by the British area code (leaving out the nought at the start) and the number you want to contact.

Methods of payment
The most common method of payment in France is the bill of exchange (*la traite*). It is usually payable at the end of the month of delivery plus sixty or ninety days.

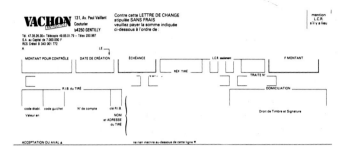

*La traite* works as follows: the supplier sends the bill of exchange to the customer for acceptance. By signing the bill the customer commits himself (it is recoverable in a French court) to paying the sum owed to the supplier on the due date. On this date, the supplier presents the bill to the customer's bank for payment. This is a form of intercompany credit which is normal practice in France. By delaying the signature, a firm can benefit from another month of credit. It is advisable to remind the customer to send the bill back if he has not done so within the customary ten days.

## SELF-ASSESSMENT

| I can | from memory (A) | with some reference to the text (B) | with full support (C) |
|---|---|---|---|
| complain about a problem | | | |
| deal with a complaint | | | |
| chase an order | | | |
| chase an unpaid bill | | | |
| count to ninety-nine | | | |
| deal with phone numbers | | | |

# 5 COPING WITH CORRESPONDENCE

## ● TASK ●

Although this chapter is about correspondence, you cannot expect to write letters at this stage. The examples given are to help you understand the correspondence you may receive. We will concentrate on oral and listening skills as well as understanding simple advertising literature and letters you may receive.

## ● ANSWERPHONES – CONFIRMATION ●

| KEY WORDS AND PHRASES | |
|---|---|
| **le répondeur** | answering machine |
| **fermer à** | to close at |
| **après la tonalité** | after the tone |
| **à la fin** | at the end |
| **vous prie d'accepter** | please accept |
| **ses excuses** | his apologies |
| **pour le retard** | for the delay |

## 5–1 I would like to confirm . . .

RÉPONDEUR    L'entreprise Ahmed ferme à 18 heures. Si vous voulez laisser un message, parlez après la tonalité. (*tonalité*)

SECRÉTAIRE    Allô, ici la secrétaire de monsieur Layen de la compagnie Norma. Je voudrais confirmer la livraison des batteries V12 à la fin de la semaine prochaine. Monsieur Layen vous prie d'accepter ses excuses pour le retard.

**EXPLANATIONS AND EXERCISES**

### Opening and closing times

To describe opening and closing times you will see or hear:

*L'entreprise **ouvre à** huit heures*    The firm **opens at** 8 am
*L'entreprise **ferme à** dix-huit heures*    The firm **closes at** 6 pm
*L'entreprise **est ouverte de** huit heures **à** dix-huit heures*    The firm **is open from** 8 am **to** 6 pm
*L'entreprise **est fermée de** dix-huit heures **à** huit heures*    The firm **is closed from** 6 pm **to** 8 am

You will also see:

*permanence de huit à dix-huit heures*    open/manned from . . . to . . .
*permanence vingt-quatre heures sur vingt-quatre*    open 24 hours

To ask at what time a firm closes or opens:

*A quelle heure fermez/ouvrez-vous?*    At what time do you close/open?
(*nous ouvrons/fermons à* . . .)

*Jusqu'à quelle heure êtes-vous ouvert?*    Until what time are you open?
(*nous sommes ouverts jusqu'à* . . .)

Other closing times:

*les congés annuels*    yearly closure (holidays)
*le congé du premier mai*    May day bank holiday

🎧    **EXERCISE 5–1**
Listen to the answerphone announcements and match the
opening or closing times with the following:

**a**  closed from 12 to
    2.30 pm

**d**  closed on Sunday

**b**  open from 7 am to 6 pm

**e**  open from 7.30 am to
    6 pm

**c**  open from 10 am to
    10 pm

**f**  closed from 12 to 2 pm

**Speak after the bip**
You might hear:

*parlez après la tonalité*
*parlez après le bip sonore*

# ● ANSWERPHONES – REQUESTING INFORMATION ●

| KEY WORDS AND PHRASES | |
|---|---|
| **le congé** | bank holiday |
| **j'ai reçu** | I have received |
| **certains produits** | some products |
| **m'intéressent** | I am interested in |
| **les conditions de vente** | sales terms/conditions |
| **mes coordonnées** | my name, address, telephone number |

## 5–2 Could you send me . . . ?

RÉPONDEUR Ici la société Paribas. Nos bureaux sont fermés
pour le congé du premier mai. Si vous voulez
laisser un message, parlez après le bip sonore.
*(tonalité)*

CLIENT J'ai reçu votre catalogue et certains produits
m'intéressent. Pourriez-vous m'envoyer la
liste des prix et les conditions de vente? Mes
coordonnées sont: monsieur Jenner,
J-E-N-N-E-R, Etablissements Lamel,
L-A-M-E-L, 15 Rue de Lille, 67 000
Strasbourg. Mon numéro de fax est le
88 60 25 57. Merci.

**EXPLANATIONS AND EXERCISES**

*Votre compagnie m'a été recommandée*   your company has
been recommended to me
*Nous sommes prêts à*   we are ready to
*Passer une commande*   place an order
*Jusqu'à*   up to/until
*Serait-il possible?*   would it be possible?
*Visiter une entreprise*   visit a firm
*Ainsi que*   as well as

**EXERCISE 5–2**

Listen to the recorded messages. Make a note of them
following the first example.

| | Name of company | Address, phone/ fax number | Contact name | Request |
|---|---|---|---|---|
| **ex** | Ets LAMEL | 15 Rue de Lille 67000 Strasbourg Fax: 88 60 25 57 | M. JENNER | • price list • sales terms |
| **a** | | | | |
| **b** | | | | |
| **c** | | | | |

## ● LETTERS ●

### KEY WORDS AND PHRASES

| | |
|---|---|
| **(pièces jointes) p.j.** | enclosures |
| **comme suite à** | following |
| **veuillez trouver** | please find |
| **ci-joint** | enclosed |
| **les prix courants** | actual prices |
| **les délais de livraison** | lead/delivery time |
| **après réception** | after receiving |
| **le bon de commande** | order form |
| **fin de mois** | end of month |
| **la facture** | invoice |
| **un escompte** | discount |
| **le paiement comptant** | immediate payment |
| **en vous remerciant** | thanking you |
| **je vous prie d'agréer** | please receive |

# Please find enclosed . . .

Here is a letter answering monsieur Jenner's request.

---

### **PARIBAS**
20 boulevard d'Arc, 14000  CAEN Cedex
tel 31 45 56 72 fax 31 65 78 54

M. JENNER
Etablissements LAMEL
v/ref. P-12            15 Rue de Lille
n/ref. LA-1           67000 Strasbourg

p.j. liste des prix        Caen, le 10 mars 1993

Monsieur
Comme suite à votre message du 9 mars, veuillez
trouver, ci-joint, la liste des prix courants.

Nos conditions de vente sont les suivantes:
— Délais de livraison: 3 semaines après réception du
  bon de commande.
— Paiement: 60 jours fin de mois de réception de la
  facture.
— Escompte de 2,5% pour paiement comptant.

En vous remerciant de votre intérêt, je vous prie
d'agréer, Monsieur, mes salutations distinguées.

Le chef des ventes

*F. Duval*

F. Duval.

## Useful phrases

Letter writing for business purposes requires a very formal style. Here are a few useful phrases:

### For acknowledgement

*Comme suite à . . .* Following . . .
*En réponse à . . .* In reply to . . .
*Nous avons bien reçu votre lettre du . . .* We received your letter of the . . .

### For enclosures

*Veuillez trouver ci-joint . . .* Please find enclosed . . .
*Nous vous adressons ci-joint . . .* We enclose . . .

### Polite phrases

*C'est avec plaisir que . . .* It is with pleasure that . . .
*Nous avons le plaisir de . . .* We have the pleasure of . . .

### For requests

*Veuillez . . .* Please . . .
*Veuillez avoir l'obligeance de . . .* We should be grateful if you could . . .
*Nous vous prions de bien vouloir . . .* Please could you . . .

### Endings

*Veuillez agréer, madame,*
*mes salutations distinguées*
*Nous vous prions d'agréer,* } Yours sincerely/faithfully
*monsieur, l'expression de nos*
*meilleurs sentiments*

Use the same form of address as used at the start of the letter:

*Monsieur* when you write to a man unless he has a title, for example *Monsieur le Directeur* or *Monsieur le Président*.
*Madame* for a woman, or *Madame la Directrice*.
*Messieurs* when you don't know whether it's a man or a woman.

# ● FAXES AND TELEXES ●

Faxes and telexes are simpler to write because you can use a more direct style and simplified expressions.

## For the attention of . . .

Here are a few examples:

### CONFIRMATION OF CHANGE OF ORDER

This is a confirmation of change of order from *les Etablissements Bourgeois* (see the conversation on page 51).

> A l'attention du service des ventes.
>
> Objet: Commande numéro 458 du six juin 1993
>
> Comme suite à notre conversation téléphonique, je voudrais confirmer le changement de la commande: pourriez-vous y ajouter 4 pièces ref. AD 352.
>
> Salutations distinguées.

### CONFIRMATION OF A HOTEL BOOKING

Mr Layen's secretary has just received confirmation from the hotel at which she made a booking.

> A l'attention de monsieur Layen
>
> Objet: réservation M. Layen
>
> Nous avons le plaisir de confirmer votre réservation: une chambre à deux lits avec salle de bain pour trois jours à partir du 21 juillet.
>
> Salutations distinguées.

Unluckily, there is an error.

🎧 **EXERCISE 5–3**

Listen to the dialogue and answer the following questions:

**a** What was the original booking?
**b** Was the error in the booking or in the confirmation?

# ● ADVERTS ●

You should not attempt to translate your advertising literature yourself. Translating technical or marketing material into French should be done by a specialist.

| KEY WORDS AND PHRASES | |
| --- | --- |
| **le salon** | show |
| **une exposition** | exhibition |
| **pour tous renseignements** | for more information |
| **s'adresser à** | contact |
| **un visiteur** | visitor |
| **un exposant** | exhibitor |
| **une demande de participation** | application form |
| **remplir** | fill in |

## Understanding adverts

### EQUIP AUTO 93

Look at the advertisement on the opposite page, about an international exhibition.

# EQUIP AUTO 93

## 11<sup>e</sup> Salon International des Equipements

1<sup>re</sup> Monte, Process, Rechange et Garage
du 22 au 28 OCTOBRE 1993
PARC DES EXPOSITIONS DE PARIS-NORD
*à 3 minutes de Roissy*
*à 20 minutes du centre de Paris par RER*

## EQUIP AUTO, LE RENDEZ-VOUS MONDIAL DES PROFESSIONS DE L'AUTOMOBILE EN EUROPE

Pour tous renseignements, s'adresser à
**EQUIP AUTO 93**
55, Quai Alphonse Le Gallo – B.P. 317
F-92107 Boulogne Cedex
Tél: 33 (1) 49 09 61 40 – Fax: 33 (1) 49 09 61 07

**EXERCISE 5–4**

After reading this advertisement, answer the following questions:

**a**  What is the exhibition about?
**b**  When does it take place?
**c**  Where does it take place?
**d**  How far is it from the Charles De Gaulle airport?
**e**  How could you get there from the centre of Paris?
**f**  Where would you write for more information?

## Asking for information

You could ask for information if you are interested:

*comme visiteur*   as a visitor
*comme exposant*   as an exhibitor

Then you will be sent:

*une demande de participation*     application form
*que vous devez remplir*     which you will have to fill in

Monsieur Layen has seen the advert (*une annonce*) and
would like more information. His secretary writes the fax:

---

Messieurs

Comme suite à votre annonce parue dans le Figaro,
veuillez avoir l'obligeance de nous envoyer une
brochure sur l'exposition internationale EQUIP AUTO
93.

Nous fabriquons des accessoires et des pièces de
rechange pour l'industrie automobile et aimerions
éventuellement exposer à votre salon.

Veuillez agréer, messieurs, nos salutations distinguées.

---

## • INVOICES •

| KEY WORDS AND PHRASES | |
|---|---|
| **le prix unitaire (PU)** | unit price |
| **hors taxes (HT)** | before tax |
| **TVA** (taxe à la valeur ajoutée) | VAT |
| **le montant** | amount |
| **TTC** (toutes taxes comprises) | tax included |
| **la traite** | bill of exchange |

# Invoice number . . .

## READING AN INVOICE

Here is an invoice from a supplier of gardening equipment:

---

**SOCIETE DUROS SA**
**Grossiste Equipement Jardin**
15, Avenue du 6 juin
14000 Caen Cedex 15

Facture n° 0235
Commande n° 458

Date: 25 juin 1992

Tél: 31 45 78 32
Fax: 31 56 23 79

E$^{ts}$ Bourgeois
67 Rue de Paris
76 009 Rouen Cedex 12

| Réf. | Désignation produits | Quantité | Prix Unit. Hors Taxes | Montant Hors Taxes |
|------|---------------------|----------|-----------------------|--------------------|
| RD 12 | Rateau | 6 | 43,10 | 258,60 |
| BR 254 | Barrière | 2 | 524,75 | 1049,50 |
| WE 45 | Tondeuse essence | 1 | 4590,95 | 4590,95 |
| AD 352 | Pelle acier | 4 | 67,35 | 269,40 |
| *Conditions de paiement*: | | Montant total | | 6168,45 |
| | | T.V.A.   17,8% | | 1097,98 |
| traite à 60 jours | | **Total** | | **7266,43** |

---

## EXERCISE 5–5

After reading the invoice, answer the following questions:

**a**  What is the invoice number?
**b**  How would you say 'product description' in French?
**c**  Does the unit price include VAT?
**d**  What is the VAT rate?
**e**  What is the method of payment?

**Formality of French correspondence**
The French are very proud of their language. They will appreciate you speaking French even with mistakes but they will not take you seriously if your written material, either letters, technical information or simple advertisements, contain spelling, structural or content errors. It is essential to employ the services of a specialist firm to translate all your technical, marketing and commercial literature.

French business letters follow a standard lay out (see page 79). The style is also important and can seem excessively flowery and long winded to an English-speaking business person. Nevertheless it is important that you respect this procedure, especially when complaining or dealing with customer complaints.

## Minitel

The Minitel is one of France's modern successes. It is a very advanced communication tool widely used by individuals and businesses.

It has two main functions:

### Telephone directory

To ensure its success, France Telecom decided to distribute the Minitel equipment (a keyboard and a screen that you just plug into a standard electric socket and connect to your phone) free of charge instead of supplying telephone directories.

### Teletel services

Minitel provides two-way communication services in a very wide variety of businesses: banking, tourism, transport, mail order, press, games etc . . . Within France most advertisements (on radio, TV and in the press) show the Minitel code.

## SELF-ASSESSMENT

| I can understand | from memory (A) | with some reference to the text (B) | with full support (C) |
|---|---|---|---|
| and leave simple answerphone messages | | | |
| simple letters | | | |
| and send simple telexes and faxes | | | |
| simple adverts to ask for more information | | | |
| invoices | | | |

# 6 WINING AND DINING

## ● TASK ●

In this unit you will learn about inviting a client to a restaurant, asking for a table, ordering a meal and asking for the bill. We will also deal with a visit to a client's house for dinner, small talk about work, travelling, family, holidays and, finally, thanking your host.

## ● INVITING A CLIENT TO A RESTAURANT ●

| KEY WORDS AND PHRASES | |
|---|---|
| **il est midi** | it is twelve o'clock |
| **l'heure du déjeuner** | lunch-time |
| **déjeuner** | to eat lunch |
| **le déjeuner** | lunch |
| **avec moi** | with me |
| **avec plaisir** | with pleasure |
| **une table** | a table |
| **pour deux personnes** | for two people |
| **vous désirez . . . ?** | would you like . . . ? |
| **la carte** | the menu |

# 6–1 Inviting a client to eat at a restaurant

| 1 🎧 | AT THE END OF THEIR MEETING |
|---|---|

M. LAYEN      Il est midi, l'heure du déjeuner. Etes-vous libre pour déjeuner avec moi?

MME BLOIS      Avec plaisir.

| 2 🎧 | AT THE RESTAURANT, ASKING FOR A TABLE |
|---|---|

SERVEUR      Monsieur-dame, bonjour.

M. LAYEN      Bonjour. Est-ce que vous avez une table pour deux personnes s'il vous plaît?

SERVEUR      Oui monsieur. Voici . . . Vous désirez un apéritif?

MME BLOIS      Non pas le midi.

SERVEUR      Et pour monsieur?

M. LAYEN      Non merci.

SERVEUR      Bien monsieur, voici la carte.

## EXPLANATIONS AND EXERCISES

**Invitation to lunch**

To invite a prospective customer to lunch or dinner you can say:

*Etes-vous libre pour déjeuner?*     Are you free for lunch?
*Voulez-vous dîner avec moi?*     Would you like to have dinner with me?
*Pourriez vous déjeuner avec moi?*     Could you have lunch with me?

For a long-standing customer you could also use:

*Nous déjeunons ensemble?*     Shall we have lunch together?
*Nous pourrions dîner ensemble*     We could have dinner together.

**Asking for a table**

You could just say *une table pour* ('a table for') followed by the number of people: *une table pour trois personnes*.

A more formal way of asking would be:

*Avez-vous une table pour trois personnes?*
*Est-ce que vous avez une table pour trois*
*personnes?*

Do you have a
table for three?

### Waiter's questions
*Vous désirez un apéritif?*   Would you like an aperitif?
*Vous voulez la carte?*   Would you like the menu?

And to ask you if you are ready to order, the waiter (*le serveur*) might say:

*Vous avez choisi?*   Have you chosen?
*Vous êtes prêts?*   Are you ready?
*Qu'est-ce que vous prenez?*   What will you have?

🎧   **EXERCISE 6–1**
Listen to dialogue 6–1 again and answer the following questions.

**a**   What time is it?
**b**   What kind of table does monsieur Layen ask for?
**c**   Is madame Blois having an apéritif?
**d**   Is monsieur Layen having an apéritif?
**e**   What does the waiter give them?

**EXERCISE 6–2**
You are phoning the restaurant Le Lion d'Or to book a table for four people for 8pm tomorrow.

| EMPLOYÉE | Allô, restaurant Le Lion d'Or, bonsoir. |
|---|---|
| YOU | *Greet her, and say you would like to book a table for four.* |
| EMPLOYÉE | Oui monsieur, pour quand? |
| YOU | *Tomorrow.* |
| EMPLOYÉE | A quelle heure? |
| YOU | *8 pm if possible.* |

| EMPLOYÉE | Alors une table pour quatre personnes demain à vingt heures, oui c'est possible. C'est à quel nom? |
|---|---|
| YOU | *Give her your name.* |
| EMPLOYÉE | Pouvez-vous l'épeler s'il vous plaît? |
| YOU | *Of course . . .* |
| EMPLOYÉE | Merci madame, au revoir. |

## ● ORDERING A MEAL ●

### KEY WORDS AND PHRASES

| | |
|---|---|
| **une entrée** | a starter |
| **vous avez choisi?** | have you chosen? |
| **une assiette de crudités** | a mixed dish of salads and raw vegetables |
| **une terrine maison** | house pâté |
| **comme plat principal** | for the main course |
| **des pommes vapeur** | boiled/steamed potatoes |
| **saignant, à point, bien cuit** | rare, medium, well-done |
| **une entrecôte grillée** | grilled rib steak |
| **des frites** | chips |
| **comme boisson** | as a drink |
| **une bouteille de vin rouge** | a bottle of red wine |
| **une carafe d'eau** | a jug of water |
| **un dessert** | a dessert |
| **le plateau de fromage** | cheese tray |
| **une glace** | ice cream |
| **une tarte aux pommes** | apple pie |

## 6–2 Ordering

| I 🎧 | ORDERING A STARTER |
|---|---|

| SERVEUR | Vous avez choisi? |
| MME BLOIS | Oui. Une assiette de crudités. |
| SERVEUR | Oui. Et pour monsieur? |
| M. LAYEN | Une terrine maison. |
| SERVEUR | Alors une assiette de crudités pour madame et une terrine maison pour monsieur. |

| 2 🎧 | ORDERING THE MAIN COURSE |
|---|---|

| SERVEUR | Et comme plat principal? |
| MME BLOIS | Un steak avec des haricots verts pour moi. |
| SERVEUR | Le steak, vous le désirez saignant, à point ou bien cuit? |
| MME BLOIS | Saignant s'il vous plaît. |
| SERVEUR | D'accord. Et pour monsieur? |
| M. LAYEN | Une entrecôte grillée avec des frites. |
| SERVEUR | Et comme boisson? |
| M. LAYEN | Une bouteille de vin rouge . . . du Bordeaux? |
| MME BLOIS | D'accord, et une carafe d'eau. |
| SERVEUR | Très bien. Une bouteille de Bordeaux rouge et une carafe d'eau. |

| 3 🎧 | ORDERING A DESSERT |
|---|---|

| SERVEUR | Vous désirez le plateau de fromages? |
| MME BLOIS | Oui merci. |
| SERVEUR | Et comme dessert? Nous avons des glaces ou une tarte aux pommes. |
| MME BLOIS | Pas pour moi merci. |
| M. LAYEN | Une tarte aux pommes. |
| SERVEUR | Très bien monsieur. |

**Starters**

*une entrée/un hors d'œuvre*   a starter

Here are a few examples of starters:

*soupe*   soup
*soupe du jour*   soup of the day
*consommé*   clear soup

*salades*   salads
*des crudités*   mixed salads, raw vegetables, and sometimes
a few slices of salami or fish
*des carottes râpées*   grated carrots
*des tomates*   tomatoes

*charcuterie*   cooked meats
*du pâté*   pâté
*la terrine maison*   house pâté
*du jambon de Parme*   Parma ham
*du saucisson/salami*   sausage/salami

*fruits de mer*   sea food
*des moules marinières*   mussels
*du crabe*   crab
*des crevettes/bouquets*   prawns/king prawns
*du homard*   lobster

*œufs*   eggs
*un œuf mayonnaise*   egg mayonnaise
*de la tarte aux épinards*   spinach flan
*une omelette aux champignons*   mushroom omelette

## Main course
The waiter could ask:

*Et comme plat principal?*   And for the main course?

You could answer:

*Je vais prendre . . .*   I'll have . . .
*Pour moi . . .*   For me . . .

And choose from the following:

*comme viande*   as meat
*un steak, une entrecôte*   steak, rib steak
*une côte de porc*   pork chop
*du gigot d'agneau*   leg of lamb
*une escalope de veau*   veal escalope/cutlet

*comme poisson*   as fish
*une truite*   trout
*une sole*   sole
*du cabillaud*   cod
*du saumon*   salmon

*comme volaille*   as poultry
*du poulet*   chicken
*du canard*   duck
*de la pintade*   guinea foul

*comme légumes*   as vegetables
*des (pommes) frites*   chips (french fries)
*des pommes de terre rôties*   roast potatoes

*des pommes vapeur*    boiled/steamed potatoes
*des haricots verts*    haricot beans

If you choose a steak, you will be asked how you like it:

*Le steak, vous le voulez comment?*    How do you want your steak?

It could be:

*bleu*    very rare
*saignant*    rare
*à point*    medium
*bien cuit*    well-done

*Un steak-tartare* is raw minced steak topped with a raw egg and spices.

## Drinks

You'll be asked: *Et comme boisson?*, 'And to drink?'.

You can choose the wine from *la carte des vins*.

*une bouteille de vin rouge*    a bottle of red wine
*une demi-bouteille de vin blanc*    a small (half) bottle of white wine
*une carafe de vin*    a jug of house wine
*un vin de pays*    a local wine

Or you could take water, *de l'eau*.

*un pichet d'eau*    a jug of water
*une bouteille d'eau minérale*    a bottle of mineral water

In French restaurants bread, *le pain*, is free.

## Cheese

Each region of France has its own cheeses (*fromages*). If you want to know about a particular one, you could ask the waiter:

*Qu'est-ce que c'est?*    What is it?
*Ce fromage, c'est quoi?*    This cheese, what is it?

You could be told:

*C'est du (fromage de) chèvre*   It is goat's cheese
*Il est doux/fort*   It is mild/strong

**Desserts and flavours**
Flavours are preceded by *au* (*à*+*le*), *à la*, *à l'*, *aux* depending on the gender of the flavour. You could order:

*une glace **au** chocolat*   a chocolate-flavoured ice cream
*une glace **à la** vanille*   a vanilla ice cream
*une glace **à l'**ananas*   a pineapple ice cream
*une tarte **aux** fraises*   a strawberry tart

| Masculine | Feminine | Word starting (with a vowel) | Plural |
|---|---|---|---|
| *au* | *à la* | *à l'* | *aux* |
| au citron | à la pistache | à l'ananas | aux fraises |

EXERCISE 6–3
Can you fill in the gaps?

**a**   une soupe ..... oignon
**b**   une soupe ..... tomate
**c**   un sandwich ..... jambon
**d**   une glace ..... orange
**e**   une tarte ..... pommes

## ● ASKING FOR THE BILL ●

| KEY WORDS AND PHRASES | |
|---|---|
| **un café** | a (black) coffee |
| **un crème** | a white coffee |
| **l'addition** | the bill |
| **le service est compris?** | is service included? |

## 6–3 Asking for the bill

AT THE END OF THE MEAL

| | |
|---|---|
| M. LAYEN | Vous prenez un café? |
| MME BLOIS | Oui merci. |
| M. LAYEN | Monsieur, s'il vous plaît? |
| SERVEUR | Oui monsieur? |
| M. LAYEN | Deux cafés et l'addition s'il vous plaît. |
| SERVEUR | Tout de suite monsieur. |

### EXPLANATIONS AND EXERCISES

**More about the bill**

To ask for the bill, just say:

*L'addition s'il vous plaît*   The bill, please

If you want to know whether service is included:

*Le service est compris?*

In most restaurants service is included and since the mid eighties, tipping, *le pourboire*, has slowly started to disappear.

**EXERCISE 6–4**

Could you get by in a restaurant? Ask for:

**a** A table for three, please.
**b** One leg of lamb, two medium steaks, please.
**c** A bottle of red wine, Bordeaux, and a carafe of water.
**d** What is that cheese? Is it mild?
**e** Two black and one white coffee.
**f** The bill, please.

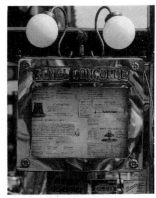

🎧　**EXERCISE 6–5**

This is a typical set meal:

---

### *Restaurant du Lion d'or*

## MENU A 145F

| **entrée au choix:** | **choice of starter** |
|---|---|
| assiette de crudités | salad |
| *ou* | *or* |
| terrine de pâté de lapin | rabbit pâté terrine |
| *ou* | *or* |
| melon glacé | iced melon |
| **plat principal au choix:** | **choice of main dish:** |
| entrecôte grillée | grilled rib steak |
| *ou* | *or* |
| escalope de veau normande | veal cutlet Normandy |
| *ou* | *or* |
| truite meunière | trout |
| **légumes du jour** | **vegetables of the day** |
| **plateau de fromages** | **cheese** |
| **dessert** | **dessert** |
| service 15% compris | 15% service included |

---

Listen to the tape. Tick what's being ordered from the menu and write down which vegetables are being ordered.

# ● AT A CLIENT'S FOR DINNER ●

| KEY WORDS AND PHRASES | |
|---|---|
| **permettez-moi** | allow me/let me |
| **ma femme** | my wife |
| **tenez** | here you are |
| **des fleurs** | flowers |
| **beau/belle** | beautiful |
| **de l'eau** | water |
| **des glaçons** | ice (cubes) |
| **et toi, ma chérie** | and you dear |
| **à votre santé/à la vôtre** | cheers |

## 6–4 At your client's house

| I 🎧 | INTRODUCTIONS |
|---|---|

MARC      Bonsoir Joseph. Ça va?

JOSEPH      Très bien merci, et vous?

MARC      Ça va. Permettez-moi de vous présenter ma femme, Colette. Colette, voici monsieur Layen de Londres.

JOSEPH      Enchanté madame.

COLETTE      Enchantée.

JOSEPH      Tenez, c'est pour vous.

COLETTE      Des fleurs, merci beaucoup, elles sont très belles.

| 2 🎧 | HAVING AN APÉRITIF |
|---|---|

MARC      Joseph, qu'est-ce que vous prenez? Un whisky, un pastis . . .

JOSEPH      Un whisky s'il vous plaît.

MARC      De l'eau, des glaçons?

JOSEPH      Un glaçon mais pas d'eau.

| | |
|---|---|
| MARC | Et toi, ma chérie, qu'est-ce que tu prends? |
| COLETTE | Un pastis s'il te plaît. |
| MARC | Voilà ton pastis et votre whisky. A votre santé! |
| COLETTE | A votre santé monsieur Layen! |
| JOSEPH | Joseph, s'il vous plaît. A la vôtre! |

**EXPLANATIONS AND EXERCISES**

### Introducing someone

To introduce someone just say: *je vous présente mon/ma collègue* for a colleague, followed by his or her name. You say *voici ma femme* for your wife, and *voici mon mari* for your husband.

You could also say:

*Permettez-moi de vous présenter . . .*    Allow me to introduce . . .

### Apéritifs

The French are very keen on *l'apéritif.* Here is a selection of apéritif drinks:

*un whisky* can be served with water, *de l'eau,* and ice, *des glaçons*
*un Pastis/Pernod/Ricard* aniseed drink served with water
*un vin cuit* fortified wine (*un martini, un cinzano, un Raphael*)
*un kir* blackcurrant juice (alcoholic) with white wine

🎧 **EXERCISE 6–6**

Listen again to the conversation at Marc's house and answer the following questions:

**a**  Which apéritif has M. Layen chosen?
**b**  Does he take water and ice?
**c**  What is Colette having?

# ● CHATTING OVER THE MEAL ●

## KEY WORDS AND PHRASES

| | |
|---|---|
| **les épinards** | spinach |
| **délicieux/délicieuse** | delicious |
| **vous parlez bien français** | you speak French well |
| **votre femme** | your wife |
| **je voyage** | I travel |
| **souvent** | often |
| **pour affaires** | for business |
| **vous êtes marié?** | are you married |
| **des enfants** | children |
| **aussi** | too/also |
| **professeur d'anglais** | English teacher |
| **goûtez ce rouge** | taste this red wine |

## 6–5 Chatting during the meal

### THIS IS DELICIOUS

| | |
|---|---|
| JOSEPH | Cette tarte aux épinards est délicieuse. |
| COLETTE | Merci Joseph. Vous parlez bien français. |
| JOSEPH | Je voyage souvent en France pour affaires. |
| COLETTE | Vous êtes marié? |
| JOSEPH | Oui et j'ai deux enfants. |
| COLETTE | Nous aussi. Votre femme travaille? |
| JOSEPH | Non. Et vous Colette, vous travaillez? |
| COLETTE | Oui, je suis professeur d'anglais. |
| MARC | Joseph, goûtez ce rouge avec le fromage . . . |
| JOSEPH | Hum . . . en effet, il est bon! |

**Family talk**
*le mari*   the husband
*la femme*   the wife
*une femme d'affaires*   a businesswoman
*les enfants*   children
*le fils*   the son
*la fille*   the daughter
*Vous êtes marié?*   Are you married?
*Je suis célibataire*   I am single
*Vous avez des enfants?*   Have you got children?
*Que fait votre mari/femme?*   What does your husband/wife do?

**Nationalities and languages**
*Marc est français et Colette est française*   (they are French)
*Joseph est anglais et sa femme est anglaise*   (they are English)
*Joseph parle anglais et français*   (he speaks English and French)
*Carlos est espagnol et il parle espagnol*   (he is and speaks Spanish)

**EXERCISE 6–7**
Can you give the nationalities of the following people and the languages they speak?

**a**  Mary        **c**  Monique
**b**  Bernt       **d**  Manuel

# ● THANKS AND GOODBYES ●

**KEY WORDS AND PHRASES**

| | |
|---|---|
| **une soirée agréable** | an enjoyable evening |
| **un repas excellent** | an excellent meal |
| **dans quelques jours** | in a few days |
| **tout le plaisir a été pour nous** | it was a pleasure |

# 6–6 Thanking your host – ending the visit

| 🎧 | SAYING GOODBYE |
|---|---|

MARC    Un dernier petit digestif?

JOSEPH    Merci non. Ce cognac est excellent mais il est tard. Merci pour une soirée très agréable et un repas excellent.

COLETTE    Tout le plaisir a été pour nous. Au revoir Joseph.

JOSEPH    Au revoir Colette.

MARC    Je vous rappelle à Londres dans quelques jours. Au revoir.

JOSEPH    D'accord. Bonne nuit.

## EXPLANATIONS AND EXERCISES

**Adjectives**

Here are some more examples of adjectives which come after the noun they describe:

*un vin rouge*   a red wine
*un steak saignant*   a rare steak
*un repas excellent*   an excellent meal

A few very common ones come before the noun:

*un bon vin*   a good wine
*un grand lit*   a double (literally 'large') bed
*un dernier petit digestif*   a last little digestif

To most adjectives describing feminine nouns add an *-e*:

*une grande bouteille*   a large bottle
*une petite bouteille*   a small bottle

But *beau*, for 'beautiful', becomes *belle*.

For the plural, adjectives normally take an *-s* at the end:

*deux steaks saignants*   two rare steaks
*trois grandes bouteilles*   three large bottles
*des fromages forts*   strong cheeses
*les belles fleurs*   the beautiful flowers

**EXERCISE 6–8**
Rewrite each sentence with the adjective in the correct form and place.

**a**  C'est un vin. (bon)
**b**  C'est une machine. (japonais)
**c**  Voilà la gamme. (complet)
**d**  Vous aimez les vins. (rouge)
**e**  Les sociétés (grand, américain)

**EXERCISE 6–9**
How would you say:

**a**  Thank you for a very pleasant evening.
**b**  The apple tart is delicious.
**c**  Thank you for an excellent meal.
**d**  You are welcome.
**e**  It was a pleasure.

## WORTH KNOWING

**Food and drink**
In recent years the three-hour lunch break has tended to disappear but it does not mean that the French have stopped taking their food seriously. A lot of shops and offices are closed between 12 and 2 pm. Negotiations started in the office will often end with the contract being signed over lunch in a convivial atmosphere. Breakfast meetings are becoming more and more popular.

Each region of France has its specialities to which local business people will be pleased to introduce you. The local wine will often be best to accompany them.

If you're invited to dinner at a client's home, you should bring flowers (avoid chrysanthemums, which in France are a sign of mourning) or chocolates for your hostess, but not wine. The French choose their wine carefully to enhance each particular dish. Don't be afraid of complimenting your host: talking about food is part of enjoying it and the French consider their cooking a worthwhile topic of conversation.

## Holidays

For the majority of French people the statutory five weeks of holidays is still split between a week in winter and four weeks in summer, either in July or August. You should avoid conducting new business during these two months.

There are eleven bank holidays (*jours fériés*):

| | |
|---|---|
| 1 January | 14 July |
| Easter Monday | 15 August |
| 1 May | 1 November |
| 8 May | 11 November |
| Ascension Thursday | 25 December |
| Whit Monday | |

When they fall on a Tuesday or a Thursday, it is customary to take the Monday or Friday off to have a four day break. This is called *faire le pont* ('making the bridge').

### SELF-ASSESSMENT

| I can | from memory (A) | with some reference to the text (B) | with full support (C) |
|---|---|---|---|
| invite a client to a restaurant | | | |
| ask for/book a table | | | |
| order a full meal | | | |
| ask for the bill | | | |
| thank my host | | | |
| talk about my family, travel … | | | |

# CAN YOU GET BY?

Try these exercises when you've finished the course. The answers are in the key to exercises.

## ● I GETTING THERE ●

a  How would you stop a man and ask him where the Underground station is?
b  How would you ask for a second class return ticket, non-smoking, to Lyon?
c  How would you say that you have a booking for two nights?
d  How would you ask for a morning call at 7.30?

## ● 2 INTRODUCTIONS ●

a  Ask to speak to monsieur Layen (on the phone).
b  Introduce yourself, your name, position and company.
c  Ask monsieur Layen if he is free on Wednesday.
d  Say you are sorry but you'd like to delay your appointment to the following Monday.
e  Say you have an appointment with madame Blois at 2 pm.
f  Say your firm manufactures spare parts and your head office is in Bristol.

## ● 3 ENQUIRIES ●

a  What would you say as you give your catalogue to your client?
b  Ask for a price list.

**c** Ask a supplier if he has item ref. 34 in stock.
**d** Ask if the prices are unit prices.
**e** Ask what the delivery time is.
**f** Order fifty parts ref. 34.

## ● 4 BUSINESS PROBLEMS ●

**a** Say the machine is out of order.
**b** Ask what's wrong.
**c** Say that you have not received the delivery.
**d** Apologise for the delay.
**e** Ask for your client's phone number.
**f** Say that your invoice has not been settled.

## ● 5 COPING WITH CORRESPONDENCE ●

**a** Say you would like to confirm the booking.
**b** The office is open from 9 am to 6 pm.
**c** Say you have received their catalogue and you are interested in some products.
**d** Ask if they could send you the current price list and sales terms.
**e** There is a three per cent discount for immediate payment.
**f** Payment is by bill of exchange, sixty days from the end of the month of delivery.

## ● 6 WINING AND DINING ●

**a** Invite a new client to lunch.
**b** Ask for a table for two.
**c** Say you'll have a mixed salad and a melon for starters.
**d** Say you'll have a steak, well-done, with French fries.
**e** Ask for a black coffee, a white coffee and the bill.
**f** Say you are married with two children.
**g** Thank your host for an excellent meal and an enjoyable evening.

# REFERENCE SECTION

## ● PRONUNCIATION GUIDE ●

By listening carefully to what is said in the recording and repeating it, you will acquire a good pronunciation. This is only a rough guide to pronunciation: it is important that you listen to the recording to get each sound right.

### VOWELS

**a**     short as in 'add' or 'lap'
*addition, salade*

**e**     ● is similar to 'a' in above
*le, de, petit*
● is similar to 'e' in 'let'
*merci, perdu, ouvert*
● *at the end of a word, is not pronounced*
*grande, petite, entreprise*
● in words ending in -er, -ez, -et, is pronounced like an *é*
*aller, prenez, pichet*

**é**     is similar to a shortened 'ay' in 'day'
*clé, entrée, déjeuner*

**è/ê**   is similar to 'e' in 'let'
*deuxième, crème, vous êtes*

**i**     is similar to 'i' in 'police'
*lit, merci, sortie*

| | |
|---|---|
| **o** | is similar to 'o' in '**o**dd' |
| | *société, prochaine, produits* |
| **ô** | is similar to 'o' in '**po**st' |
| | *hôtel* |
| **u** | (difficult because it has no equivalent in English) |
| | is close to the 'ew' of 'thr**ew**' |
| | *une, tu, je suis, réunion* |
| **ai** | is similar to *é* |
| | *français, anglais, s'il vous plaît* |
| **ei** | is similar to *è* |
| | *renseignement* |
| **oi** | is pronounced 'wa' |
| | *Blois, droite, bonsoir, moi* |
| **au** | is similar to *o* |
| | *gauche, au revoir, automobile* |
| **ou** | is pronounced 'oo' |
| | *vous, nous, bonjour* |

## NASALS

These are vowel sounds followed by an *-n*. (Pinching your nose while saying these sounds will give you an exaggerated reproduction.)

| | | |
|---|---|---|
| **1** | **-in** | *vin, quinze* |
| | **-un** | *un billet, un ticket* |
| | **-ain** | *train, pain* |
| **2** | **-ien** | *bien, combien* |
| | **-oin** | *joindre, à point* |
| **3** | **-en** | *ventes, trente, prendre* |
| | **-an** | *changer, quarante* |
| **4** | **-on** | *bon, livraison, nous allons* |

## CONSONANTS

A consonant at the end of a word is not pronounced: *vous prenez, petit, grand, français*. The exceptions are those words ending with *-c, -l* and *-ur*, for example: *avec, il, pour, sur*.

The following consonants sound the same in French and in English:

*b, d, f, k, m, n, p, s, t, v, z*

The following are slightly different:

| | |
|---|---|
| **c** | + *a, o, u* or a consonant is like 'c' in '**c**at' <br> *continuez, café, classe* |
| **c** | + *e* or *i* is like 's' in '**s**ignal' <br> *merci, voici, en face* |
| **ç** | is like 's' in '**s**ignal' <br> *ça va, français* |
| **ch** | is like 'sh' in '**sh**oe' <br> *changez, chambre, douche* |
| **g** | + *a, o, u* or a consonant is like 'g' in '**g**ap' <br> *gauche, grand, garanti, catalogue* |
| **gn** | is like 'n' in 'o**n**ion' <br> *renseignement, agneau* |
| **h** | is not pronounced <br> *hôtel, heure* |
| **j** | is like 's' in 'plea**s**ure' <br> *je, joindre* |
| **ll** | after an 'i' is like 'y' in '**y**es' <br> *bouteille, grillé* |
| **ph** | is like 'f' in '**f**ish' <br> *téléphone* |

**qu**    is like 'k' in '**k**ilo'
*qu*atre, *qu*elle heure, *qu*alité

**r**    comes from the back of the throat
pa*r*don, me*r*ci, *r*etou*r*, d*r*oite

**t**    followed by -*ion* is pronounced 's'
sta*tion*, produc*tion*, addi*tion*

## ACCENTS

Accents change the pronunciation but also the meaning of some words. We have already seen in this section how the different accents change the pronunciation of the letter *e*.

When spelling, they are named:

**é**    e, accent aigu

**è**    e, accent grave (or **à**: a, accent grave)

**ê**    e, accent circonflexe

**ë**    e, tréma

On the other vowels, the *accent circonflexe* makes the sound of the vowel deeper and longer:

**a**    as the 'a' in 'l**a**p'

**â**    as the 'a' in 'p**a**st'

The *tréma* does not alter the sound of the vowel but means that it is independent and must be pronounced as it is in the alphabet:

**ï**    as 'i' in 'pol**i**ce'
*mais* is pronounced like a short 'May' and means 'but'
*maïs* is pronounced as ma-iss ('ma' of 'map' and 'iss' of 'miss'), and means 'maize'

# ● NUMBERS ●

| | | | |
|---|---|---|---|
| 0 | *zéro* | 30 | *trente* |
| 1 | *un* | 40 | *quarante* |
| 2 | *deux* | 50 | *cinquante* |
| 3 | *trois* | 60 | *soixante* |
| 4 | *quatre* | 70 | *soixante-dix* |
| 5 | *cinq* | 71 | *soixante et onze* |
| 6 | *six* | 72 | *soixante-douze* |
| 7 | *sept* | 73 | *soixante-treize* |
| 8 | *huit* | 80 | *quatre-vingts* |
| 9 | *neuf* | 81 | *quatre-vingt-un* |
| 10 | *dix* | 82 | *quatre-vingt-deux* |
| 11 | *onze* | 90 | *quatre-vingt-dix* |
| 12 | *douze* | 91 | *quatre-vingt-onze* |
| 13 | *treize* | 100 | *cent* |
| 14 | *quatorze* | 101 | *cent un* |
| 15 | *quinze* | 102 | *cent deux* |
| 16 | *seize* | 200 | *deux cents* |
| 17 | *dix-sept* | 201 | *deux cent un* |
| 18 | *dix-huit* | 300 | *trois cents* |
| 19 | *dix-neuf* | 1000 | *mille* |
| 20 | *vingt* | 1001 | *mille un* |
| 21 | *vingt et un* | 1230 | *mille deux cent trente* |
| 22 | *vingt-deux* | 1 000 000 | *un million* |
| 23 | *vingt-trois* | 1 000 000 000 | *un milliard* |

# ● DAYS OF THE WEEK ●

| | | | |
|---|---|---|---|
| *lundi* | Monday | *vendredi* | Friday |
| *mardi* | Tuesday | *samedi* | Saturday |
| *mercredi* | Wednesday | *dimanche* | Sunday |
| *jeudi* | Thursday | | |

# ● MONTHS OF THE YEAR ●

| | | | |
|---|---|---|---|
| *janvier* | January | *juillet* | July |
| *février* | February | *août* | August |
| *mars* | March | *septembre* | September |
| *avril* | April | *octobre* | October |
| *mai* | May | *novembre* | November |
| *juin* | June | *décembre* | December |

# ● COUNTRIES ●

| | | | |
|---|---|---|---|
| *l'Allemagne (f)* | Germany | *la Grèce* | Greece |
| *l'Angleterre (f)* | England | *la Hollande* | Holland |
| *la Belgique* | Belgium | *l'Italie (f)* | Italy |
| *le Canada* | Canada | *l'Irlande (f)* | Eire |
| *la Chine* | China | *le Japon* | Japan |
| *le Danemark* | Denmark | *le Luxembourg* | Luxemburg |
| *l'Ecosse (f)* | Scotland | *la Norvège* | Norway |
| *l'Espagne (f)* | Spain | *le Pays de Galles* | Wales |
| *les Etats-Unis* | USA | *le Portugal* | Portugal |
| *la Finlande* | Finland | *la Russie* | Russia |
| *la France* | France | *la Suède* | Sweden |
| *la Grande-Bretagne* | Great Britain | *la Suisse* | Switzerland |

# KEY TO EXERCISES

## ● I GETTING THERE ●

### 1–1 Directions
**a** WC (les toilettes) ● **b** Bagages ● **c** RER

### 1–2 More directions
**a** Hôtel ● **b** Gare ● **c** Banque ● **d** Métro

### 1–3 Time
1 **e** ● 2 **a** ● 3 **c** ● 4 **d** ● 5 **b**

### 1–4 Buying a train ticket
**a** Lyon
**b** a single (*un aller simple*)
**c** no, second (*deuxième*)
**d** no (*non fumeur*)
**e** 16.14
**f** carriage (voiture) 12, seat (place) 20
**g** 260 Francs

### 1–5 Booking into a hotel
Bonsoir madame, j'ai réservé une chambre, monsieur Sandell.
C'est bien ça.
A quelle heure servez-vous le petit déjeuner?
Pourriez-vous me réveiller à six heures trente s'il vous plaît?
Merci et au revoir madame.

# ● 2 INTRODUCTIONS ●

## 2–1 On the phone
Je voudrais parler à monsieur Vardon.
Je voudrais/puis-je parler à monsieur Vardon s'il vous plaît.
Quand puis-je le joindre?
Je rappellerai après quinze heures.
Merci et au revoir monsieur.

## 2–2 Introductions
**a** Je suis/je m'appelle Roger Vadim, je suis chef des ventes de la
    société Ferguson.
**b** Je voudrais un rendez-vous.
**c** Je voudrais vous présenter nos produits.
**d** D'accord, vendredi prochain je suis libre à quatorze heures.
**e** Au revoir monsieur/madame, à jeudi.

## 2–3 Dates
1 **c** ● 2 **d** ● 3 **a** ● 4 **e** ● 5 **b**

## 2–4 Delaying an appointment
**a** the following Monday (le lundi suivant)
**b** he is not free (je ne suis pas libre)
**c** Wednesday 16 (le mercredi seize)
**d** at 3 pm (à quinze heures)

## 2–5 At reception
Bonjour madame, j'ai un rendez-vous avec madame Delmas.
Je suis monsieur Sandell de la société Sameco.
Merci madame.
Enchanté madame.
Très bien, pas de problèmes.
Merci madame.

## 2–6 Towns and countries
**a** Notre siège social est à Londres en Angleterre.
**b** Notre siège social est à New-York aux Etats-Unis.
**c** Notre siège social est à Paris en France.
**d** Notre siège social est à Tokyo au Japon.
**e** Notre siège social est à Berlin en Allemagne.

# • 3 ENQUIRIES •

### 3–1 My, your, our
**a**  voici mon billet
**b**  voici ma carte de visite
**c**  voici mon catalogue
**d**  voici mes produits
**e**  voici votre clé
**f**  voici vos pièces de rechange
**g**  voici votre petit-déjeuner
**h**  voici notre catalogue
**i**  voici nos produits
**j**  voici notre gamme complète

### 3–2 We sell, we have . . .
**a**  C'est ça, nous vendons des pièces de rechange.
**b**  C'est ça, nous avons un catalogue.
**c**  C'est ça, nous garantissons nos produits.
**d**  C'est ça, nous offrons la gamme complète.
**e**  C'est ça, nous travaillons en France.

### 3–3 Spelling
1 **c**  •  2 **a**  •  3 **d**  •  4 **e**  •  5 **b**

### 3–4 I am going to . . .
**a**  Non mais je vais être libre demain.
**b**  Non mais je vais avoir un rendez-vous demain.
**c**  Non mais je vais regarder le catalogue demain.
**d**  Non mais je vais réserver une chambre demain.

### 3–5 Enquiring about stock availability
**a**  parts ref. AD 352 (référence AD trois cent cinquante-deux)
**b**  ten (dix)
**c**  four (quatre)
**d**  6 June, order number 458 (la commande du six juin, numéro quatre cent cinquante-huit)
**e**  by telex (par télex)

### 3–6 Match the discounts
1 **b**  •  2 **d**  •  3 **a**  •  4 **e**  •  5 **c**

### 3–7 Understanding the discounts offered
**a**  items ref. DB 120 and CF 435 (DB cent vingt, CF quatre cent trente-cinq)

**b** 50 for 5% and 100 for 9% (cinquante pièces pour 5%, cent pièces pour 9%)
**c** the discount for a first order over 50 (escompte pour une première commande supérieure à cinquante pièces)
**d** a fortnight (quinze jours)

### 3–8 More dates
1 **c** ● 2 **d** ● 3 **b** ● 4 **a** ● 5 **e**

### 3–9 Placing an order
**a** Je voudrais vingt pièces de rechange référence TR cent cinquante-six.
**b** Nous comptons sur la livraison dans quinze jours.
**c** Je vous envoie le bon de commande immédiatement.

# ● 4 BUSINESS PROBLEMS ●

### 4–1 Me, you . . .
**a** Je m'appelle Pierre.
**b** Je vais me renseigner.
**c** Je vous rappellerai.
**d** Je voudrais vous présenter nos produits.
**e** Pourriez-vous me réveiller à sept heures?

### 4–2 Complaining about a problem
**a** Le téléphone ne marche pas.
**b** La machine est en panne.
**c** C'est la mauvaise taille.
**d** Ce n'est pas la bonne qualité.

### 4–3 Perfect tense: I have done something
**a** Mais j'ai confirmé la commande hier.
**b** Mais j'ai réservé une chambre hier.
**c** Mais j'ai regardé votre catalogue hier.
**d** Mais j'ai pris le train hier.
**e** Mais j'ai parlé au PDG hier.

### 4–4 Apologising
**a** Je suis désolé, je suis en retard.
**b** Veuillez nous excuser, c'est une erreur.
**c** Malheureusement, il est trop tard.
**d** Excusez-moi, je vais me renseigner.

### 4–5 Matching phone numbers
1 **b** ● 2 **d** ● 3 **e** ● 4 **a** ● 5 **f** ● 6 **c**

### 4–6 Leaving a message
Je voudrais parler à monsieur Platini s'il vous plaît.
Quand puis-je le contacter?
Oui merci. J'attends toujours la dernière livraison.
Monsieur Sandell.
C'est le 081 837 2564.
Merci et au revoir madame.

### 4–7 Negatives
**a** Je n'ai pas réservé une chambre à deux lits.
**b** Vous n'avez pas remplacé les articles.
**c** Nous n'avons pas reçu la livraison.
**d** Il ne m'a pas rappelé hier.
**e** Elles n'ont pas envoyé la commande.
**f** La facture n'a pas été réglée.
**g** Je n'ai pas commandé ça.

# ● 5 COPING WITH CORRESPONDENCE ●

### 5–1 Opening and closing times
1 **b** ● 2 **a** ● 3 **e** ● 4 **d** ● 5 **f** ● 6 **c**

### 5–2 Recorded messages

|   | Name of company | Address, phone/ fax number | Contact name | Request |
|---|---|---|---|---|
| **a** | Société Bontemps | 219 Avenue de la Paix 59000 Lille | Monsieur Carpentier | ● catalogue ● liste des prix |
| **b** | Garages Braek et Fils | Bruxelles Tél: 56 63 24 89 | Monsieur Braek | ● rendez-vous pour première commande |
| **c** | Société Baron | Hotel Royal Park Fax: 071 547 2830 | Madame De La Vaquerie | ● visiter notre entreprise |

### 5–3 I would like to check
**a** two single rooms with bathrooms for three nights from the 21 July (deux chambres à un lit avec salle de bain pour trois nuits à partir du 21 juillet)
**b** in the confirmation (dans la confirmation)

### 5–4 Understanding a written advert
**a** car equipment (l'équipement automobile)

**b** from 22 to 28 October 1993 (du 22 au 28 octobre 1993)
**c** Paris-Nord Exhibition centre (au parc d'exposition de Paris-Nord)
**d** three minutes (trois minutes)
**e** by RER (par RER)
**f** Equip Auto 93
55 Quai Alphonse Le Gallo, BP 317
F 92107 Boulogne Cedex

## 5–5 Reading an invoice

**a** 0235
**b** désignation produits
**c** No (Prix unitaire Hors Tax)
**d** 17.8%
**e** draft within sixty days (traite à 60 jours)

# ● 6 WINING AND DINING ●

## 6–1 Inviting a client to a restaurant

**a** midday (midi/12 heures)
**b** a table for two (une table pour deux personnes)
**c** no, not at midday (non, pas le midi)
**d** no (non)
**e** the menu (la carte)

## 6–2 Booking a table

Bonsoir madame, je voudrais réserver une table pour quatre personnes.
Demain.
Vingt heures si possible.
Mike Sandell.
Bien sûr, SANDE deux L.

## 6–3 Fill in the gaps: au, à la . . .

**a** à l'  ●  **b** à la  ●  **c** au  ●  **d** à l'  ●  **e** aux

## 6–4 Could you get by in a restaurant?

**a** Une table pour trois s'il vous plaît.
**b** Un gigot d'agneau, deux steaks à point s'il vous plaît.
**c** Une bouteille de vin rouge, du Bordeaux, et une carafe d'eau.
**d** Ce fromage, qu'est-ce que c'est? Il est doux?
**e** Deux cafés et un crème.
**f** L'addition s'il vous plaît.

## 6–5 Ordering from the 145F menu
**entrées**: 1 melon glacé et 2 terrines de pâté de lapin.
**viande**: 2 escalopes de veau et une truite meunière.
**légumes**: 1 haricots verts, 1 frites, 1 pommes vapeur et 2 salades.

## 6–6 Choosing an aperitif
**a**   a whisky (un whisky)
**b**   ice but no water (un glaçon mais pas d'eau)
**c**   a pastis (un pastis)

## 6–7 Nationalities and languages
**a**   Mary est anglaise et elle parle anglais.
**b**   Bernt est allemand et il parle allemand.
**c**   Monique est française et elle parle français.
**d**   Manuel est espagnol et il parle espagnol.

## 6–8 Adjectives
**a**   C'est un bon vin.
**b**   C'est une machine japonaise.
**c**   Voilà la gamme complète.
**d**   Vous aimez les vins rouges.
**e**   Les grandes sociétés américaines.

## 6–9 Thanking your host
**a**   Merci pour une soirée très agréable.
**b**   La tarte aux pommes est délicieuse.
**c**   Merci pour un repas excellent.
**d**   Je vous en prie.
**e**   Tout le plaisir a été pour nous.

# ● CAN YOU GET BY? ●

## 1  Getting there
**a**   Pardon monsieur, la station de Métro s'il vous plaît?
**b**   Un aller-retour, deuxième classe, non fumeur, pour Lyon s'il vous plaît.
**c**   J'ai une réservation pour deux nuits.
**d**   Pourriez-vous me réveiller à sept heures trente s'il vous plaît?

## 2  Introductions
**a**   Je voudrais parler à monsieur Layen.
**b**   Je suis Mike Sandell, chef des ventes de la compagnie Sameco.

**c**  Vous êtes/êtes-vous libre mercredi?
**d**  Je suis désolé, je voudrais remettre notre rendez-vous au lundi suivant.
**e**  J'ai rendez-vous avec madame Blois à quatorze heures.
**f**  Nous fabriquons des pièces de rechange et notre siège social est à Bristol.

## 3 Enquiries
**a**  Voici notre catalogue.
**b**  Avez-vous/je voudrais la liste des prix?
**c**  Avez-vous l'article référence trente-quatre en stock?
**d**  Ce sont les prix unitaires?
**e**  Quels sont les délais de livraison?
**f**  Je voudrais cinquante pièces référence trente-quatre s'il vous plaît.

## 4 Business problems
**a**  La machine est en panne.
**b**  Qu'est-ce qui ne va pas?/Quel est le problème?
**c**  Nous n'avons pas reçu la livraison.
**d**  Veuillez nous excuser du retard.
**e**  Quel est votre numéro de téléphone?
**f**  Notre facture n'a pas été réglée.

## 5 Coping with correspondence
**a**  Je voudrais confirmer la réservation.
**b**  Le bureau est ouvert de neuf heures à dix-huit heures.
**c**  J'ai reçu votre catalogue et certains produits m'intéressent.
**d**  Pourriez-vous m'envoyer la liste des prix courants et les conditions de vente?
**e**  Il y a une remise de trois pour cent pour paiement comptant.
**f**  Paiement par traite, soixante jours fin de mois de livraison.

## 6 Wining and dining
**a**  Etes-vous libre pour déjeuner avec moi?
**b**  Une table pour deux personnes s'il vous plaît.
**c**  Nous prenons une crudités et un melon en entrée.
**d**  Je prends un steak, bien cuit, avec des frites.
**e**  Un café, un crème et l'addition s'il vous plaît.
**f**  Je suis marié et j'ai deux enfants.
**g**  Merci pour un repas excellent et une soirée agréable.

# WORD LIST

## A

*accepter* to accept
un *accessoire* accessory
d' *accord* OK
*accorder* to grant
l' *acier (m)* steel
l' *addition (f)* the bill
les *affaires (f)* business
*agréable* pleasant/enjoyable
*agréer* to receive
*aimer* to like
*ajouter* to add
un *aller-retour* a return
un *aller simple* a single
*allô* hallo (phone)
*alors* then
*américain* American
un *an* year
un *ananas* pineapple
*anglais* English
l' *Angleterre (f)* England
un *apéritif* pre-meal drink
à l' *appareil* speaking (phone)
je m' *appelle* my name is
*après* after
un *article* item
*asseyez-vous* sit down
une *assiette* plate
une *assurance* insurance
un *atelier* workshop
*attendre* to wait

*aujourd'hui* today
*aussi* also
en *avance* early
*avec* with

## B

des *bagages (m)* luggage
*bain (m)* bath
une *barrière* gate
une *batterie* battery
*beau (belle)* beautiful
*beaucoup* (very) much
*bien* well
*bien sûr* of course
un *billet* ticket (train)
*blanc(-he)* white
*bleu* blue/rare (steak)
une *boisson* drink
*bon(-ne)* good
un *bon de commande* order
  form
*bonjour* good morning/
  afternoon
*bonne nuit* good night
*bonsoir* good evening/
  night
un *bouquet* king prawn
une *bouteille* bottle
un *bureau* desk/office

## C

les *cadres* managerial staff
*ça va* fine
*ça fait* it comes to (price)
du *cabillaud (m)* cod
un *café* coffee
du *canard (m)* duck
une *carafe* carafe/jug
des *carottes râpées (f)* grated
    carrots
la *carte* menu
une *carte de visite* business card
*cassé* broken
un *catalogue* catalogue
une *cerise* cherry
*c'est* it is
*certains* some
une *chambre* room
un *champignon* mushroom
un *changement* change
*changer* to change
*chargé* charged
un(e) *chef* manager
    *chef des ventes* sales
      manager
    *chef des achats* buying
      manager
*chéri(-e)* dear
du *chèvre* goat's cheese
du *chocolat* chocolate
*choisi* chosen
*ci-joint* enclosed
un *citron* lemon
une *classe* class
une *clé* key
*combien* how much/many
une *commande* order
*commander* to order

*comme* as
*comment* how
*comment allez-vous?* how
    are you?
une *compagnie* company
*complet* full
*composter* to validate
*comprendre* to understand
*compris* understood
la *comptabilité* accountancy
*comptant* immediate
    (payment)
*compter sur* to expect/rely
    on
une *conférence* conference
*confirmer* to confirm
un *congé* bank holiday
les *congés annuels* main
    holiday
*contacter* to contact
*continuer* to continue
un *contremaître* foreman
*contentieux* legal
les *coordonnées (f)* details
    (name, address, tel.,
    fax)
une *côte de porc* pork chop
*courant* actual, current
un *crème* white coffee
une *crevette* prawn
des *crudités* mixed salad
*bien cuit* well done (steak)

## D

le *Danemark* Denmark
*dans* in
le *déjeuner* lunch
le *petit-déjeuner* breakfast

*un délai de livraison* lead/
delivery time
*délicieux(-se)* delicious
*demain* tomorrow
*dernier* last
*dès que* as soon as
*une désignation* description
*que désirez-vous?* what would
you like?
*désolé* sorry
*deuxième* second
*devant* in front of
*vous devez* you must/are
supposed to
*le dîner* dinner
*dire* to say
*disons* let's say
*dites-lui* tell him/her
*donc* so/therefore
*donner* to give
*une douche* shower
*doux(-ce)* mild
*la droite* right
*à droite* on the right

---

**E**

*de l' eau (f)* water
*en effet* indeed/actually/yes
*l' emballage (m)* packaging
*enchanté* pleased to meet
you
*endommagé* damaged
*un(e) enfant* child
*ensemble* together
*une entrecôte* rib steak
*une entrée* entrance, starter

*une entreprise* firm
*l' entretien (m)* maintenance
*envoyer* to send
*épeler* to spell
*des épinards (m)* spinach
*une erreur* error
*une escalope de veau* veal cutlet
*un escompte* discount
*l' Espagne (f)* Spain
*l' essence (f)* petrol
*est* is
*les établissements* firm
*les Etats-Unis (m)* USA
*été* been
*éventuellement* possibly
*exactement* exactly
*excusez-moi* excuse me
*exposer* to exhibit
*une exposition* exhibition

---

**F**

*fabriquer* to manufacture
*en face* opposite
*une facture* bill/invoice
*une faute* fault
*une femme* wife/woman
*une femme d'affaires*
businesswoman
*fermé* closed
*fermer* to close
*une fille* daughter/girl
*un fils* son
*la fin* end
*une firme* firm
*une fleur* flower
*fort* strong

*une fraise* strawberry
*français* French
*franco domicile* free delivery
*des frites (f)* chips
*du fromage* cheese
*fumeur* smoking

## G

*la gamme* range
*garanti* guaranteed
*à gauche* on the left
*la gauche* left
*le gérant* manager
*du gigot d'agneau* leg of lamb
*une glace* ice cream
*un glaçon* ice cube
*goûter* to taste
*grand* big/large
*grillé* grilled
*un grossiste* wholesaler

## H

*des haricots verts* haricot beans
*l' heure (f)* time/hour
*hier* yesterday
*du homard* lobster
*un homme* man
*un homme d'affaires*
   businessman
*un hors d'œuvre* starter
*hors taxes (HT)* before tax

## I

*ici* here

*immédiatement*
   immediately
*l' industrie automobile* car
   industry
*ça m' intéresse* I'm interested in it
*l' intérêt (m)* interest

## J

*du jambon* ham
*le Japon* Japan
*japonais* Japanese
*joindre* to reach
*un jour* day
*jusqu'à* up to/until

## L

*là-bas* over there
*laisser* to leave
*lesquels* which ones
*libre* free
*une ligne* line
*une liste des prix* price list
*un lit* bed
*une livraison* delivery
*lui* to him/to her

## M

*madame* Mrs
*mademoiselle* Miss
*en magasin* in stock
*le magasin* shop/warehouse
*malheureusement*
   unfortunately
*marcher* to work
*un mari* husband
*marié* married

un *matin* morning
*mauvais* bad/wrong
*merci* thank you
*mettre* to put
*midi* midday
*moi* me
un *mois* month
*mondial* world wide
*monsieur* Mr
le *montant* amount
des *moules (f)* mussels

## N

*naturellement* of course/
  naturally
une *navette* shuttle
un *nom* name
*non* no
*noté* noted
*nouveau(-elle)* new
une *nuit* night
un *numéro* number

## O

un *œuf* egg
un *oignon* onion
une *orange* orange
*ou* or
*où* where
*oui* yes
*ouvert(-e)* open
un *ouvrier* worker
*ouvrir* to open

## P

un *paiement* payment
une *panne* breakdown

en *panne* broken down
*pardon* excuse me
*parfait* perfect/fine
*parler* to speak
*partir* to leave
un *passant* passer-by
*passer* spend (time)
*patientez* wait/hold on
les *Pays-Bas (m)* Holland
une *pelle* shovel
une *permanence* opening hours
*permettez-moi* allow me
une *personne* person
le *petit-déjeuner* breakfast
je *peux* I can
une *pièce* part
une *pièce de rechange* spare part
*pièces jointes (p.j.)*
  enclosures
de la *pintade* Guinea fowl
á la *pistache* pistachio
  flavoured
une *place* seat
un *plaisir* pleasure
un *plat* dish
un *plateau* tray
à *point* medium (steak)
une *pomme* apple
une *pomme de terre* potato
des *pommes vapeur* boiled
  potatoes
une *porte* gate/door
du *poulet* chicken
*pour* for/to/in order to
*pourrait-il?* could he?
*pourriez-vous?* could you?
*pouvoir* to be able to/can
*pratique* handy
*premier* first

*prendre* to take
*prenez* take
*présenter* to introduce
*prêt* ready
*prévenir* to let know/to warn
*prévu* planned
*je vous en prie* you're welcome
*principal* main
*pris* taken
un *prix* price
un *problème* problem
*prochain(e)* next
la *production* production
un *produit* product
un *professeur* teacher
*puis* then
*puis-je?* may I?

## Q

*qu'est-ce que?* what?
*quand* when
*que* that
*quel* which
*quelques* a few
*ne quittez pas* hold on (phone)
*quoi* what

## R

un *rabais* discount/reduction
*rapide* fast
*je rappellerai* I'll call back
un *rateau* rake
*à la réception* on receiving
*recevoir* to receive
*reçu* received

un *reçu* receipt
*regarder* to look at
*régler* to settle
*regretter* to regret
*remerciant* thanking
*remettre* to delay/postpone
une *remise* discount
*remplacer* replace
un *rendez-vous* appointment
un *renseignement* information
*renseigner* to give information
*se renseigner* to look for information
un *repas* meal
un *répondeur* answerphone
une *réservation* booking
*réserver* to book
*responsable de* in charge of
*rester* to stay
*en retard* late
un *retard* delay
une *réunion* meeting
*réveiller* to wake up
*au revoir* goodbye
*rôti* roasted
*rouge* red

## S

*saignant* rare (steak)
un *salon* show/trade fair
la *santé* health
du *saucisson/salami* salami
du *saumon* salmon
*je ne savais pas* I didn't know
le/la *secrétaire* secretary
une *semaine* week

*un serveur* waiter
*servez-vous?* do you serve?
*un service* department/service
*le siège social* head office
*s'il vous plaît* please
*une société* company
*une soirée* evening
*une sortie* exit
*sortie d'usine* factory price
*la soupe du jour* soup of the
   day
*souvent* often
*le standard* switchboard
*le/la standardiste* switchboard
   operator
*en stock* in stock
*succès* success
*je suis* I am
*suite à* following
*suivant* following
*supérieur(-e)* greater

## T

*TTC* all taxes included
*TVA* VAT
*une table* table
*une taille* size
*tard* late
*un tarif* price list/rate
*une tarte* pie
*tenez* here you are
*une terrine maison* house terrine
*les toilettes (WC)* toilets
*une tomate* tomato
*une tonalité* bip/tone

*une tondeuse* mower
*tôt* early
*toujours* always/still
*tout, tous* all
*tout à fait* absolutely
*tout droit* straight on
*un train* train
*une traite* bill of exchange
*un transporteur* carrier
*travailler* to work
*trouver* to find
*une truite* trout

## U

*unitaire* unit (price)

## V

*en vacances* on holiday
*je vais* I am going
*la vanille* vanilla
*vendre* to sell
*venir* to come
*veuillez* please
*de la viande* meat
*du vin* wine
*voici* here is/here are
*voilà* there is/there are
*une voiture* car/carriage
*je voudrais* I would like
*vouloir* to want
*un voyage* journey
*voyager* to travel
*vraiment* really

## Y

*y* there